Furry Fairy Tails

PD the Pug's Bedtime Stories

By PD the Pug

(With help from Mommy Marilee Joyce)

Illustrations by Maria Vyasene

Furry Fairy Tails: PD the Pug's Bedtime Stories

Copyright © 2025 by Marilee Joyce
Illustrations by Maria Vyasene

Printed in the United States of America

Paperback ISBN: 978-1-965253-35-9
eBook ISBN: 978-1-965253-36-6

To the fairest maiden in all the land
my Fawn Girl Pug Crush
One day I will carry you away to our pug palace
where we will live happily ever after

INTRODUCTION

"Oooooh, PD! This is so *exciting*, isn't it? What do you think happens *next?* Do you think the prince will find Cinderella? Do you think the wicked stepsisters will ruin everything? Do you think love will win, PD? Or evil? Let's see what *happens!* Can you stand the *suspense*, PD?"

I'm snuggled up in Mommy's snuggy warm lap, listening to her read a story about some girl who wears rags and has a mean stepmommy and mean stepsisters and the girl goes dancing with a prince and she is wearing slippers made out of glass and then something about a clock announcing it is nigh-nigh curfew time and then she tries to run in the glass shoes to some crazy pumpkin car driven by a mouse, but before she gets to the mouse's car, one of the slippers slips off and then the prince finds it and that's where we are!

And, okay, it *is* pretty exciting. But it's also sorta silly—because I can't drive, so how could a mouse?

This story time thing is new for me. Mommy has started reading to me at night before putting me to bed because she believes this will cure my alleged "nighttime anxiety." A couple of months ago, I heard her telling the vet that I was getting into mischief at bedtime—stuff like chewing on the cuddle chair silk pillow that I'm not allowed to play with, making a poopie on the (in my defense) very grass like green rug in the dining room, and barking at my reflection in the sliding glass door. Stuff like that. Stuff like that especially at nigh-nigh time, when I am supposed to have sleepy face like I want to go to bed.

The phone was on speaker, so I heard the vet say that anxiety at night can mean a dog needs more exercise (no!) or a new toy (yes!) or an extra bedtime snack (double yes!!) or maybe music therapy (huh?). The vet said not to worry, though, because I am fit and healthy, and she said it's probably "just a phase" and that it might just be "PD being PD and seeking more attention."

(Excuse me, but I am a celebrated author! Attention seeks *me!*)

So I know that Mommy is convinced about this "anxiety" thing, but the truth of the matter is that during my walkies, I keep seeing my nemesis Ralph the Dog (see all previous PD the Pug series books) sniffing around *my* secret fawn girl pug crush. So, when Mommy and I get home from our roam, all I do is *think, think, think* about that wretched cur flirting with my girl! So excuse *me* if I am a wee bit wound up in the evening! I am not "anxious," Mother! Any angst you sense, any disquietude, jitters, twitches, shakes, heebie-jeebies or other seeming signs of distress is just me plotting, planning, scheming to vanquish that fleabag!

Alas, Mommy and the vet have decided I need "calming activities and calming treats" to get me in the mood to snooze. So, for the past couple of months, Mommy has been giving me a nightly chicken-flavored hemp chew and—in lieu of the music therapy idea—reading me bedtime stories.

Mommy very nearly ordered me a ThunderShirt. According to Rover.com, there is science behind these lightweight "anxiety wraps"; they Velcro snugly around a dog's chest and abdomen, offering continuous pressure "akin to a hug." But Mommy hasn't tried that yet because she knows I don't dig costumes (see *No, YOU Sit! PD the Pug's Manual for How to Train Your Human,* chapter six).

Every evening after dinner, I get my nightly CBD treat, and then Mommy gets out her old book of fairy tales and scoops me onto her lap for story time. So far, we have read about little pigs and queens and poisoned apples and paupers and frog princes and lots of other interesting things. Many of the tales have monsters and ogres and gremlins and tons of suspense, and I don't really get how that's supposed to help me sleep. But I have to admit I love this special Mommy lap time.

As Mommy continues reading me the tale of pretty Cinderella who I hope ends up marrying the prince, I begin to relax. Between the hemp chew and the romantic story, I am able to fret a bit less about wicked Ralph and his attempts to woo *my* princess. And then, as that Mr. Sandman guy—who takes you away at nigh-nigh time and nappy time—makes my eyelids feel heavy, I imagine that my secret fawn girl pug crush is Cinderella and I am Prince PD come to sweep her away to my kingdom, and Ralph is . . . well, we could borrow the poisoned apple from that other story. But I am benevolent, so I don't poison him, I just put him in a dungeon or something for a while. Something like that.

As I drift away to Slumberland, far from Mommy's soft voice, far from my worries over Ralph, the last thought I have is that I could write a better version of this tale . . . a version that casts me as the hero and Ralph as the vanquished villain and ends with my secret fawn girl crush and me living happily ever after. In fact . . . I bet I could write better versions of every fairy tale ever written. They'd be the most fantastical fables from the most masterful make-believe manufacturer: *me!* I'll be PD the Pug, the Bard of Bedtime.

So, all you humans, come snuggle up to PD, and I'll tell you a story. . . .

Chapter One

THE UGLY PUGLING

Once Upon A Time in a land called Arlington, Virginia, there lived a little black pug puppy named PD. He had been adopted from a happy place called Howling Hill Kennels by a nice woman he called Mommy. His baby days were a time of pure joy as Mommy fed and cuddled and bathed and played with him.

Mommy's human family and friends would visit, and all who came would ooh and aah over little PD.

"Such a perfect puppy!" they'd proclaim. "Such a divine dog!" they'd declare. "Such a splendorous specimen!" they'd speak. "Such an anointed animal!" they'd announce. All were in agreement that little PD was the most adorable dog they had ever set eyes upon.

It came to pass that time passed and a new pastime was bestowed to the now-three-month-old pug. His vaccinations had made his immune system mighty and strong, and so his veterinarian deemed little PD ready to go on his first walk. Mommy packed a handful of treats, two poopie bags, and a portable rubber bowl and a bottle of water for on-the-go drinks, and off they went! PD and Mommy ventured into the neighborhood and the great beyond.

The outdoors was a world heretofore unknown to little PD. All around him were new things: bushes and trees and flowers and sidewalks and fire hydrants and scents and smells and odors and aromas.

And other dogs. Lots and lots of other dogs.

Until this moment, PD had only left Mommy's castle in a pet carrier. So he had thought he was the only dog in the land, and that the only other beings were human beings. Now he was seeing dog beings! Other *dogs*! All these other *dogs*! All these potential furry friends! All these other creatures that were like him! Just like PD!

Except . . . they weren't.

PD couldn't put his toe on it, but as he stared at the other canines, he sensed there was a difference between them and him. Something subtle, something slight, something small. But clearly it was something that, for whatever reason, caused every dog he passed to turn up its nose.

Worse, as PD and Mommy continued their stroll, PD noticed that every dog they passed was laughing at him. Some snickered and sniggered. Some giggled and guffawed. Some chortled and chuckled. One cackled and convulsed. PD didn't understand the merciless mocking. And despite

Mommy tossing him treats and excitedly pointing out things of interest along the walk—"Such pretty flowers, PD!" . . . "Look at that bluebird, PD!" . . . "What a tall tree, PD!"—he felt a cloud of sadness on this cloudless Spring day.

Why are the other dogs taunting and teasing me? PD pondered. *Why don't any of them want to play with me? Why won't they let me sniff them? Why aren't they grooming me with licks? Why aren't they wagging their tails at me?*

Why don't they like *me?? What is it about me? What* IS *it?*

Mommy and PD continued their trek, stopping at a park where humans and their dogs were enjoying games with balls and Frisbees, sharing treat time, and laughing up a storm.

PD tried and tried to join in, going from one dog to the next. PD noticed that while all the humans were friendly to him— "Hey, little buddy!" . . . "Want a head pat, little pug dog?" . . . "Let's get a selfie with you, me and your mommy!"—the dogs were another story. They just couldn't stop nudging one another, pointing at PD, and shrieking in laughter.

Just as PD was mustering up the courage to ask the other dogs what about him was so funny, a dog whose dog tag said *Ralph the Dog* nodded at a group of eight or so other dogs. Then they all surrounded PD and broke out in a cruel chorus, finally making clear what they found so hilarious:

> Flat face pug! Flat face pug! There's no snout on
> his flat-faced mug!
> He doesn't have a schnozzle! How can he take a
> whiff?

He doesn't have a nozzle! How can he even sniff?
Flat face pug! Flat face pug! There's no snout on
  his flat-faced mug!

On and on they sang, much to the mortification of poor little PD. Adding to his humiliation was the fact that Mommy—who didn't speak dog language and assumed the dogs were barking words of welcome and friendship—was clapping along to the yelps and dancing around PD with that sweet Mommy smile on her pretty Mommy face.

PD could hear the words, but—this being his first walk and his first meetup with other dogs—he just couldn't understand what they meant. He was a dog, just like them! He was furry just like them! He liked frolicking and running around and peeing on bushes and rassling and roughhousing and jumping up and down and all around just like them!

And he could smell just *fine*, thank you very much. *What do they mean I can't whiff and sniff?* he wondered. *I have a nose! I can whiff and sniff with the best of them!*

I can whiff and sniff like there's no tomorrow! I can smell the smells and sniff the sniffs as well as any dog here. There's nothing wrong with my nose! I'm just like them! Just like them! Just like them!

But even as he had the thought, PD sensed he was wrong. And as clapping, dancing Mommy waved a happy goodbye to the group of taunters, two words from the dogs' chant hit him:

Flat face. Flat face. *Flat. Face.*

As realization dawned that, *yes,* maybe something *was* dissimilar, disparate, noticeably different between him and them, PD tugged so hard on his leash that Mommy had to grab onto a thick branch of a nearby tree so as not to topple over. PD ran—with Mommy jogging along virtually on his very tail—to a large puddle of water left on the sidewalk from the previous night's rainfall. Nervously, he leaned forward to see his reflection.

And there it was: his flat face.

It's true, PD thought, staring at the reflection of a cute but snout-less pug. *I look different. I look special, and not the good kind of special like when Mommy says I am so special to her.*

No, this is a bad *special,* thought PD. *A* yucky *special. An* ugly *special.* Tears rolled off his pug nose and plopped onto his likeness in the puddle.

I am ugly. I am an Ugly Pugling.

"PD? You okay, little sweetie?" asked Mommy, a concerned look on her face as her usually overly zippy, zestful, zinging-about dog sat unusually still. "You just made lots of new friends who seemed to be yapping up a storm with you. I'd have thought you'd be doing your happy zoomies all over the place."

But PD was so sad, he couldn't even meet Mommy's questioning eyes, couldn't bear to look into her concerned face. No. Because, like a nightmare replaying over and over in his mind, he just kept imagining mean Ralph the Dog leading that pack of dogs as they circled around him and jeered and cheered and laughed and chanted about his flat face.

After a long moment of staring at his face and thinking of his lack of a snout, PD finally lifted his round head away from the puddle and looked past Mommy to the wider world beyond the park.

No wonder no one wanted to play with me, mused the little pug mournfully. *I'm revolting, repulsive, a repugnant pug. Ugly Pugling! Ugly Pugling! Ugly Pugling!*

PD frowned. *No dogs like me,* he thought. *No dogs want to be my friend. They think I'm ugly. The Ugly Pugling. They don't want me around. No one wants me around.*

Suddenly, as a perplexed and then shocked and then panicked Mommy looked on, PD mustered all his PD strength and yanked so hard against his leash that the handle flew from Mommy's hand. The restraint no longer restraining him, PD raced away, running as fast as his little pug legs could carry him.

I'm not staying where I'm not wanted, he thought angrily as he tore through neighborhood after neighborhood. Forcing himself to not be emotionally moved by the slowly fading cry of "PD! PD! Where are you going, PD? PD! Come back!" as poor frantic Mommy wailed and shouted and hollered behind him, PD dashed away, focused on putting more and more distance between himself and the scene of his mortification and pain.

On and on he sprinted, barely aware of the stares from the humans he passed, barely noticing the trees, flowers, bushes, houses, hydrants, hose bibs, street signs, and other common sights that a very uncommon-feeling PD sailed past.

Finally, when his little limbs let him know they couldn't take any more, PD slowed to a walk, at last taking note of his surroundings. He didn't know where he was; he just knew he was nowhere near the *bad* park and the *bad* dogs and the *bad* event.

Already PD was missing Mommy terribly, but he fought off a brief urge to run back to her. *I won't go back,* he sulked. *I might feel lonely without Mommy and her nice human friends and family, but I'd rather be alone forever than ever go on another walkie and go through what I went through today.*

Up ahead, about a block away, PD spied another park. Panic overtook his little body, and he found himself wishing night would fall so his black coat would help conceal him, help him be a bit less noticeable to any cold-hearted canines that might spot him and break into another chorus of cruelty.

PD's round pug head swiveled and his body swirled as he searched for a place to hide. Just as he was preparing to sprint off, he noticed movement at the park. Four-footed movement. From lots of four-footed movers.

Oh no! Dogs! Lots of dogs! And they're heading my way!

PD just knew this was going to go the way it had gone at the other play place, with PD trying to make friends and the other dogs wanting nothing to do with him because of his flat face. He tilted his head down, hiding his pug nose from what he sensed were at least a dozen pairs of curious dog eyes, and prayed they would pay him no mind, just go about their business and do their doggie business and not get into *PD's* business!

Alas, it was not to be. Although he had hung his head so low he was nearly lying down, PD could see a dozen sets of paws gathering around him. He gritted his canine canines and prepared for whatever heartless harmony was about to fill the air, whatever sadistic song was about to break out regarding what they would surely deem PD's strange face.

But when the silence continued, PD mustered his courage and lifted his head . . .

And took in the most amazing sight he could ever have imagined. And "imagined" felt like an apt explanation, as PD at first thought he was hallucinating. He had to be, right?

All around PD were other flat-faced dogs. Like him but not *quite* like him. Some of them had longer or shorter legs, slimmer or beefier bodies, sleeker or fluffier coats, or longer, shorter, straighter or stubbier tails than PD did. But they all had flat countenances just like PD's. They all seemed happy and kind. They all were smiling and panting and wagging their tails at PD, who, although confused, cautiously wagged his tail in response.

"I'm Beulah Boxer," said the flat-faced dog closest to PD.

"I'm Shelton Shih Tzu," said the flat-faced dog next to Beulah.

"And I'm Lulu Lhasa Apso," said the flat-faced dog just behind Shelton.

"I'm Terry Boston Terrier." . . . "I'm Jacqueline Japanese Chin." . . . "I'm Charles Chow Chow." . . . "I'm Nathan Neapolitan Mastiff." . . . "I'm Allen Affenpinscher." . . . "I'm . . ." . . . "I'm . . ." . . . "I'm . . ." . . . "I'm . . ."

A stunned PD swung his head back and forth, staring into each flat face, each normal, natural, *beautiful* flat face surrounding him as, one after the next, his new friends introduced themselves. *Wow! Look at all these snout-less dogs!* he thought happily. Boxer! Boston terrier! Cane corso! French bulldog—and another bulldog! Dogue de Bordeaux! Brussels griffon! Bull mastiff! Chinese shar-pei and more! So many dogs! So many *flat-faced* dogs. Yes! Dogs whose noses were just like flat-faced PD's.

"Hi, everyone," said PD, showing them his snaggliest snaggletooth grin. "My name is PD. PD Pug."

And the other snout-less dogs welcomed PD into the group, befriending him in the way he earlier had so hoped the snouted dogs would do.

But then PD grew serious. He had to address what was troubling him. He braced his backbone and bravely asked:

"I hope you don't take this the wrong way, but all of you are missing a snout, just like me. There were all these dogs at the park down the way who laughed at me and taunted me, even broke out in an impromptu, improvised, very *impolite* tune about the oddity of not having a snout."

Now PD looked down in embarrassment. "They made me so sad, made me feel so bad about myself that I broke free of my Mommy and raced all the way here. I didn't want to stay where I wasn't welcome."

PD turned his head away to hide the tears beginning to well in the inner corners of his big googly eyes. "They, um . . . they made me feel ugly. Like the Ugly Pugling or something."

The many flat-faced dogs who were circled around PD looked at one another and then back at PD. One of them— Beulah, the boxer—nuzzled PD's head to get him to turn back to her and the group.

"Oh, PD, you are just perfect," said Beulah. "Perfectly flat-faced, just as all pugs are, just as all pugs are supposed to be. Just like all us flat-faced breeds are supposed to be. You're beautiful, PD, absolutely beautiful."

Charles Chow Chow chimed in. "Plus, PD, that bullying sounds just like something this cur named Ralph the Dog and his gang of snout-nosers would do. Don't let him get to you."

"Yeah," Allen Affenpinscher added. "You're as great as we all are, as all your new friends are. Ralph could only wish he was as wonderfully perfect as you."

"You guys," Lulu Lhasa Apso lightheartedly lectured, "Ralph and his snout-nosed pals are perfectly made, too. We all are perfect just the way we are!"

The group of flat-faced friends looked at one another and nodded in agreement. Even PD—who still was feeling the sting from the earlier teasing he experienced—joined in, bobbing his round head up and down.

Then Beulah Boxer yipped, "One thing, though: snout-nosed or not, Ralph is a cur!"

The group broke into howls of laughing barks. After nuzzling all his new pals, PD ran off toward home. He was now a happy and confident flat-faced pug, eager to show Mommy and the world his newfound belief in himself.

But despite the pride he felt, and as eager as he was to get home to what he knew would be a very worried Mommy, he really wished he didn't have to go past that other park again. The last thing he wanted was to run into Ralph the Dog and his band of miscreants. Unfortunately, it was the only route home PD knew.

He had run for several blocks when the park suddenly loomed before him. Just as PD had feared, he could make out Ralph and his friends surrounding some other poor pup. Hoping to pass them without being noticed, PD kept his round head tilted down as he ran past, focused on just getting home.

Alas.

"Whoa, whoa, whoa there!" Suddenly Ralph and his gang were blocking PD's way. "If it isn't good ol' Flat-Face. Where do you think you're going, Flat-Face?"

Considering the number of menacing-looking, sneering dogs surrounding him, PD easily could have given into fear and assumed a submissive stance. But no! He summoned the memory of Beulah Boxer and all the other new friends and recalled their adjective for PD.

PD squared his square pug body and faced Ralph the Dog square on.

Ralph opened his maw. But before he could resume his taunting, PD said:

"My name isn't Flat-Face. It's PD. And, yes, I *am* flat-faced. *Perfectly* flat-faced. Perfectly flat-faced PD."

Neither Ralph the Dog—who was staring stupefied—nor his horde of heavies barked a bullying word. As nervous as PD felt inside, he forced himself to stand tall and look intently into Ralph's eyes. The eye-lock challenge ended moments later when Ralph sensed his dog pack retreating behind him.

"C'mon, Ralph," a particularly long-snouted borzoi called from the exiting group. "Let's find some other snub-noser, one who doesn't yet know he's just as good as us.

"Too bad PD already figured out that we all smell and sniff the delights of the world the same."

Ralph the Dog gave PD one more scowl—which the newly brave PD took in stride—and ran to catch up with his ring of rascals. PD looked on with a big grin, feeling better than he had all day.

Then PD realized how late it was. *Oh no! It's almost dark!* he fretted. *Mommy will be beside herself. I must get home!*

Just as he started his sprint, he suddenly froze, rooted to his spot in the center of the park. Before him, just to the left of a stately elm tree and just a tiny bit to the right of a pretty bed of pink and white impatiens, was a sight more beautiful than PD would have believed existed.

A fawn girl pug. A gorgeous fawn girl pug. A *flat-faced,* gorgeous fawn girl pug.

PD was in love. He knew that from that moment on, his heart was stolen, forever owned by this perfect pretty pug. He merely needed to meet her, and then, like a knight in shining armor, he'd whisk her away and they'd be together forever.

But not right now! thought the suddenly very shy PD. *Not today!*

PD felt much too shy to approach a creature so lovely. He felt as handsome as a knight thanks to his new flat-faced friends, but his courage was still shy of knight status. In fact, PD even momentarily wished a big-nosed dog would come along so he could hide behind his snout!

Thanking his lucky stars that this flat-faced beauty was more interested in peeing against the elm tree than in noticing her new admirer, PD quickly made a beeline out of the park and toward home. His stride was peppier than usual thanks to the happy thoughts of a future with his new secret fawn girl pug crush.

As PD bolted back toward home, he was lost in reverie, envisioning one story after another about his flat-faced queen and the brood of flat-faced pug puppies they would one day create. He hoped his Mommy would be fine with letting everyone live with her. Maybe she would even build them a big pughouse behind her townhouse with plenty of big trees to mark and a big playpen full of toys and a big treat room and also . . .

"PD! PD! There you are, my sweet, sweet PD! I've been worried sick!"

So deeply lost in thoughts of his future with the betrothed of his fantasies, PD hadn't seen Mommy dashing down the street toward him. He looked up and into her wet eyes, then snapped out of his daydream and jumped into her waiting arms.

"Oh, PD. You're back!" Mommy exclaimed. "Why did you look so sad back there at the park? Were those dogs being mean? I thought they were trying to howl along with you."

If only you knew, PD thought.

As he looked up into Mommy's happy face, PD suddenly realized something he hadn't before now:

Mommy's nose was small like a button.

No wonder Mommy adopted me from Howling Hill! thought PD. *She's a snub-nose, too!* And he made a little snicker-snort noise, the one that always made Mommy smile.

As PD snuggled in Mommy's arms and stared into her pretty Mommy face with its pretty button nose, PD saw her break into a grin. But it was a wider grin than he would have expected from a single PD snicker-snort.

Mommy turned so PD could see in the direction whence he had come—and PD saw that all his new flat-faced pals had followed him home, human parents in tow.

"We wanted to make sure you got home okay, PD," said Nathan Neapolitan Mastiff. "You really tore out of there! But now we see why. Our mommies and daddies worry too when we run off!"

After nuzzles and licks all the way around, PD let Mommy lead him home.

"Oh, PD, now I understand," said Mommy. "You didn't see other flat-faced dogs at the first park, and you felt different."

PD wagged his tail and grinned his snaggletooth grin.

"Silly PD," said Mommy. "You are the most beautiful doggie in the world. Beautifully, perfectly different and beautifully, perfectly you—just like every dog is perfectly them.

"Those big-snouted dogs have nothing on you, PD."

Well, other than a silly snout, PD laughed to himself as they headed to their happy home.

(PD note: This PD Fairy Tail is based on "The Ugly Duckling" by Hans Christian Andersen. The moral of the tale is that we should not judge a book—or, in this case, a dog—by its cover, but rather by its values, qualities and treatment of others. Even when it wee-wees on the white rug. Even when it gets free of its leash at the vet's and chases a very scared cat around and around the lobby and down the hallway. Even when it digs up all the pretty flowers that were just planted that morning. Even when it growls so loud at Ralph the Dog on walkies that Ralph's mommy gives its mommy a stern talking-to. Even then.)

Chapter Two

THE PUG PIPER OF ARLINGTON

𝔑𝔬𝔴 𝔍𝔱 𝔠𝔞𝔪𝔢 𝔗𝔬 𝔓𝔞𝔰𝔰 that the metropolis of Arlington was suffering from a great cat infestation. There were countless cats, incalculable on any calculator, mewling and moaning and munching up every morsel in sight. Everywhere one looked, the furry felines were filching fish, mooching milk, cadging chicken, and just grabbing every goodie and nipping every nibble they could put their paws on. The townsfolk despaired of how to rid the area of these odious, odorous, obnoxious, beastly beasts.

Outside the town hall, Arlington's citizens crowded the commons and demanded that something be done. So to appease the cantankerous, cranky, cross constituents, Mayor Michael, Mr. Big of the municipality, promised to pay one hundred bags of baubles to anyone able to alleviate the purrers' pandemonius pother and purloining of provisions. News of the reward quickly spread as the denizens demanded deliverance.

Erelong there appeared a mysterious magical-pipe-toting black pug named PD the Piper. Introducing himself to the mayor and his council, PD the Piper claimed he was a crackerjack cat catcher who could rid the municipality of its mountains of monstrous meowers.

Mayor Michael skeptically eyed the fleabag's flute as he considered whether the hound was a hustler or a true cat capturer. After consulting with Town Treasurer Tammy, the mayor offered to trade the trinkets for the ouster of the tabbies.

"Mr. PD the Piper," Mayor Michael declared, the doubt drawn on his facial features, "one hundred gleaming gems will be yours—but only if you rid Arlington of every one of those cats!"

Considering for all of three seconds how much his Mommy would love those jewels, PD the Piper told Mayor Michael that no self-respecting dog would accept bling as bounty, but that he would do the job if the reward were changed to one hundred bags of bully sticks.

There commenced murmurs and mutterings between Mayor Michael and Treasurer Tammy before the latter nodded at the furry flautist. "Very well, PD the Piper," the treasurer stated. "One hundred bags of bully sticks for the purging of the pussycats. And I do mean every last one! Out of this town!

"Now, get to it!"

And off PD the Piper went, visions of bully stick gnawing and nibbling, chomping and chewing filling the round brain in his round bean. He was so lost in thought that he nearly ran smack into his pal Beulah Boxer.

"Oh, hi PD! That's quite a pipe you've got there!" Beulah exclaimed. "Are you in a band? I knew this New Guinea Singing Dog once named Norman who was famous for singing and howling. I didn't know pugs were among the melody makers."

(PD note: According to Dogster.com, the New Guinea Singing Dog is one of eleven breeds of dogs that "sing." And no, pugs didn't make the cut. However, I am exceptional at barking at my own reflection.)

"Good to see you, Beulah!" PD said, holding out his instrument to allow his friend a closer look. "This is my magical music maker. The town council is paying me a hundred bags of nummy bully sticks to get the cats out of here."

"Wow, yeah, so many crazed cats!" said Beulah. "For a while I was having a ball chasing them all over the place, but golly, now it's like they've taken over! Good thing you and your toy are going to clear them out."

PD patted the pipe, eyeing his pal. "It's not a *toy*, Beulah. It's *magical.* It's a magical musical device. You'll see." And with that—after the friends gave one another's rumps a sniff—PD went off to find and force out the felines.

The "finding" part didn't take long. The kitties were everywhere: on the streets, in the trees, in the parks, in the schoolyards, in every business's parking lot, on the rooftops, in the gutters, in the alleyways, on every fence and wall. Everywhere! Everywhere! The cats were everywhere! Arlington was completely crawling with cats!

But while the townsfolk fretted, PD the Piper headed into the meowing maelstrom with confidence. Hoisting his magic flute above his pug head to show the crowd of kitties the instrument that was to play their swan song, PD the Piper turned in a full circle and took in the reality of this serious situation.

These cruddy cats don't know what's about to hit them, he thought. *I'm the musical magician! I'll lure and charm and entice and tempt and coax those cats and then, HA! My magical tooter will transform into a . . .*

Suddenly, from the corner of one googly eye, PD the Piper spied a clowder of cats eyeing him from the roof of the Council Hall. As the frontmost felines leaned over the rooftop to stare at what they saw as a town intruder, the self-named magic mutt saw dozens and dozens more cats crowding behind them.

And that's just one rooftop! PD the Piper considered. *Truly, the tabbies are taking over the town!*

The rooftop cats grew curiouser and curiouser about this flute-ferrying foreigner, until they all leapt down—landing on their paws with no pain, as cats do—and surrounded PD the Piper. Moments later, as if things were not crowded enough, hundreds more pussycats were pussyfooting toward PD the Piper, coming from every path, passage, and parkway in what was clearly now a meow-nicipality! Within moments, PD the Piper was hemmed in on every side. Cats! Cats! Cats!

The cats crept ever closer. PD the Piper's googly eyes reached their very googliest as he found himself in the eye of a furry hurricane. The cats caterwauled and cried, meowed and mewled, yowled and howled. *No matter,* he mused. *No amount of mousers is too many for me—PD, the Piper—to subdue. These milk munchers are no match for my magic!*

Just as the felines figured they had made clear to this new-comer who was the boss around this town, PD the Piper hunched up on his haunches and brought the magical pipe to his maw. Unsure of what was about to happen, the cats arched their backs and puffed up their fur, swishing their tails, hissing and spitting. No way would they allow this pug to presume he was going to put pressure on the self-pro-claimed padrones of this place!

Unperturbed, PD the Piper puffed into his magical pipe. What happened next absolutely captivated the cats—because out of the flute floated none other than the rockabilly band Stray Cats! As band leader Brian Setzer produced his guitar and began to strum, the thousands of stray cats controlling Arlington couldn't help but line up in a cat conga line as the song began:

Ooh-ooh, ooh-ooh
Ooh-ooh, ooh-ooh . . .
Black and orange stray cat sittin' on a fence . . .

The cats' eyes glazed over as they became more and more entranced. They were so bewitched by Setzer's Gretsch that, as one, they began to twitch!

. . . I strut right by with my tail in the air . . .

As the stupefied miles-long line of felines looked on, PD the Piper again brought the pipe to his mouth, and out flew thousands of ginormous stereo speakers! The devices quickly stationed themselves in every section of the city, ensuring every cat in the metropolis could make out the melody:

Stray cat strut, I'm a ladies' cat
I'm a feline Casanova, hey man, that's that
Get a shoe thrown at me from a mean old man
Get my dinner from a garbage can . . .

Even PD the Piper—who knew the cats were mere moments from terrorizing the town no more—couldn't stop himself from dancing and spinning in circles, chasing his curly pug tail. His merriment was just slightly muted upon the sudden arrival of Mayor Michael and his sidekick Treasurer Tammy, who came to check on the chucking of the cats.

The officials watched as the awestruck cats stared at Brian Setzer and bandmates in dumbfounded wonder. PD the Piper took their distraction as his cue to up his magic game. Into the magical pipe he blew as the Stray Cats sang:

. . . Meow!

Yeah, don't cross my path . . .

. . . I don't bother chasing mice around . . .

. . . I got cat class and I got cat style . . .

And then, out of the magical pipe came miles and miles of magical catnip.

Knowing the already stupefied strays were now his, PD the Piper watched as the catnip floated above those furry heads, stretching from one end of the city-long conga line to the other. One paw in front of the other, the cats—now befuddled by catnip—began to strut to the strains of "Stray Cat Strut." But what they couldn't know was that they were traipsing their way clean out of town. And not just out of town, but to their own cat world . . .

Or rather, *the* Cat World. Because before the cats, the town officials or even the conjured-up rockabilly trio knew what was happening, PD the Piper blew a final big note with his mysterious flute and . . . *Voilà!*

Seemingly as one organism, the conga line of kitties flew into the air and became a furry whirling whirlwind! The whirlwind grew and grew and then *whoooooooosh!* In an instant, it sailed across the country and then across the Pacific Ocean and deposited its entire cat load . . .

Onto Cat Island! While the dog instinct in PD the Piper might have wanted to make Arlington's cats just disappear, the kindhearted pug decided they could have a happy life far from the municipality. So off they went to the island of

Aoshima, Japan, popularly known as Cat Island, where cats outnumber people six to one. And now thanks to PD the Piper, by thousands more! So at the same moment Arlington was waving a gleeful goodbye to the cats, Japan was greeting them with a hearty "Hello Kitty(s)!"

(PD note: No need for readers to worry about the well-being of the cats on Cat Island. According to that Wikipedia guy, food donations come in from all over Japan. And as for the cats' health, Catster.com says mainland veterinarians visit the island regularly.)

The next morning, PD the Piper—a bit sleepy from spending half the night wide awake, spinning in circles thinking of the one hundred bags of bully sticks on which he'd soon be chewing, chomping and champing—headed to Mayor Michael's office.

On the way, he couldn't help but notice the number of Arlington residents out and about, enjoying their day. Everyone looked smiley and at peace. PD the Piper squared his withers and proudly wiggled his haunches, knowing he was the reason the citizens had finally exited their dwellings. He was their hero, the one who had captured and cleared out the cats.

You're welcome! thought the proud pug as he smilingly strutted into the mayoral office's reception area.

"Ah! You must be the famous PD the Piper!" exclaimed a pleasant-looking woman seated behind a desk. "Mayor Michael is at a breakfast meeting, but he left something for you. Make yourself comfortable, and I'll go retrieve it!"

PD the Piper could barely contain himself from doing zoomies all over the office. He was so excited to get his yummy reward! One hundred bags of bully sticks! One hundred bags of bully sticks! One hundred bags of bully sticks!

"And here you go, Mr. Piper! I bet you are thrilled to get such a great reward for your bit of work!"

Wait. What?? Where is the rest of it?? fumed the petulant pug to himself as he stared at the outstretched arm bearing not the promised one hundred bags of bully sticks . . . not even one bag of bully sticks . . . but one sad, solitary stick. This clearly misguided woman was holding aloft one lousy bully stick! And it wasn't even wrapped!

"Bit" of work?? the peeved piper seethed, glaring at the woman proffering the solitary stick. *I performed a magical miracle! I cleared out the cats! Every last one, just as I was told! I did my part! Where is the reward I was promised??*

Noting that her guest was none too happy, the receptionist patted his head and said, "Yes, well, Treasurer Tammy said something to Mayor Michael like, 'Well, Mr. Mayor, PD the Piper merely puffed on his pipe. It's not like he deserves more than one bully stick for that ounce of effort.' Plus, the money we would have spent on the one hundred bags of bully sticks now can go toward our salary increases . . ."

With a trace of pity in her voice, she added, "Sorry, Mr. Piper, but one bully stick is sufficient. Nothing more can be done. Good day to you."

PD the Piper angrily accepted the single stick and exited, slamming the door behind him. *Nothing can be done, eh? Oh, something can be done, all right. Something* will *be done, all right!*

Focused on his fury, PD the put-out piper nearly stumbled over Beulah Boxer.

"Whoa there, PD!" Beulah said as she leapt out of his way. "What's with the frowny face?"

"Those lousy leaders misled me!" PD cried. "They promised me a hundred bags of bully sticks to rid the town of the cats, and then they broke their word! They lied to me!"

"Well, you sure did get the cats out," Beulah agreed. "This certainly is one tabby-less town. Sorry, PD. But I guess even one bully stick is something to be happy about."

PD stared at Beulah. "But they promised me one hundred bags. They all but stole my treats! So, I will steal theirs! Mayor Michael and Treasurer Tammy will rue the day they cheated PD the Piper!"

And with that, the magical-pipe-bearing PD the Piper stomped off, tossing the now-unwanted bully stick to his friend as he went. He had *just* the justice to mete out of the crooked criminals who had robbed him of his rightful reward.

Smiling smugly, PD the Piper blew into his magical flute. Suddenly a ginormous garbage bag emerged from the flute's end. It grew and grew, becoming ginormouser and ginormouser, until it separated from the instrument and went flying off... off to grocery stores, restaurants, bakeries, convenience shops, and anywhere else that supplied food to Arlingtonians, swooping in and filling itself with every morsel.

Next the pipe blew out a huge hand, as big as a mountain. Lightning-quick, the hand reached into every home, removing anything edible (unless it was meant for animals, of course). And finally, the magical flute became a phone and called every single food distributor and deliverer that had been scheduled to deliver to the area and canceled all requests.

Not a crumb of consumables could be counted. Nary a nosh could be noted. Not one delectable could be detected.

There. Was. No. Food!

His pipe now securely back in his paws, PD the Piper took in the scene around him. People were still exiting their homes, but this time it was not to rollick and romp and revel over the cat clearance. Rather, they had come out to gripe about the rumbling and roiling of their empty bellies.

"Police! Police! Someone call the police!" proclaimed one portly man from his doorway as he clutched his stomach. "All my food is gone!"

A woman racing frantically around the yard next door chimed in. "Ours, too! My boy was biting into his burger when *shazam*—a huge hand reached through the window and snatched it! Then it emptied out the fridge and the pantry!"

And on and on it went. Every town member told similar tales. Finally the news reached Mayor Michael and Treasurer Tammy—ironically, just as the magic hand was preventing an Uber Eats driver from delivering their lunch! Into the mayor's inner sanctum ran the receptionist, the woman who had met PD the Piper earlier that morning. "Mayor Michael! Treasurer Tammy! The townsfolk are in an uproar! There's no food! No food! No food!"

"What's this madness, Shirley? What are you babbling and blathering on about?" the mayor demanded of his underling.

"Yes, yes, out with it already," an annoyed Treasurer Tammy added impatiently. "And where is the Uber Eats man with our delicious steaks?" she asked, envisioning the arrival of the expensive ribeye made possible by her shrewd shirking of the promised payment to the poor Piper.

"That is just it. There is no Uber Eats delivery. There will *be* no steak," the chastised secretary explained. "That PD the Piper apparently took all our food and deactivated our deliveries. Something about revenge for not getting his promised reward for getting rid of the cats!"

The mayor and the treasurer stared at one another with eyes nearly as googly as PD the Piper's orbs at their googliest. "Well, go find him, Shirley! Don't let him get away! We need our food back!"

Shirley raced out the door and ran smack into Beulah Boxer, who was peaceably enjoying a bowl of kibble on the town commons. All around her, dogs savored their suppers while Arlington's humans went hungry.

"Oh, Beulah!" shrieked Shirley. "Help us! Find PD the Piper! He took all the human food as punishment for being stiffed. Beulah, please! Fetch the Piper! Tell him the mayor wants to see him!"

Hmmm, thought Beulah. *That's what you get for crossing a cat-capturing canine. But I guess I can at least see if PD will take a mayoral meeting.*

Half an hour later, a tuckered-out Beulah Boxer found PD the Piper, who was about to board a metro train and head to his home. Beulah explained the situation, and, against his better judgment, PD said he'd take a meeting with the officials.

PD picked up his pipe, and Beulah Boxer led him back to the town hall. Shirley the receptionist raced off to get Mayor Michael and Treasurer Tammy, who—as they entered the outer office and sat on either side of their guest—were now warily watching, wondering whether PD the Piper was going to perform some other perturbing prank with his pipe.

"Now then, Mr. Piper!" the mayor began. "Surely you can't expect a hundred bags of bully sticks for such a simple bit of work. We need that money in our treasury!"

"Be reasonable, Mr. Piper!" the treasurer tossed in. "We have obligations! We have—"

"You have bloated salaries! And bloated bellies," Shirley suddenly shouted, surprising her bosses. "I know you are going to fire me, but I can't not say this! You stole that Pug Piper's promised prize! You were wrong! Wrong! Wrong!"

As gobsmacked Mayor Michael and slack-jawed Treasurer Tammy were struck dumb by the sudden boldness of heretofore shy and subservient Shirley, PD the Piper and Beulah Boxer howled at the hilarity of the situation. PD the Piper noted the Uber Eats menu open to the expensive steak restaurant and snorted and was about to turn on his paw and leave when the mayor spoke:

"Oh, very well, very well! You are right, of course, PD the Piper! You rid us of those cats . . . yes, yes, you deserve more of a reward. Tell you what! How about—"

"One! One bag of bully sticks!" Treasurer Tammy interjected. "One bag is a lot of bully sticks! Surely that is more than fair!"

PD the Piper, Beulah Boxer, and Shirley the receptionist all rolled their eyes. Then they chuckled and began walking out.

"Oh crud!! Okay, okay, wait! You win! You can have your full reward, Mr. Piper," the treasurer said. "I guess we have no choice if we don't want to go as hungry as we would have had we let the Piper go. We were wrong to not pay up."

"Plus," the mayor added, his gluttonous side rearing its head, "perhaps if we hurry, we can catch that Uber driver."

Moments later, his one hundred bags of bully sticks secured to his sturdy pug back, PD the Piper reversed the curse, willing his magical pipe to return all the food to Arlington's pantries, patisseries, and other purveyors of human food. Everyone was happy and fed and full.

Except for Shirley, who the mayor had just fired. So PD the Piper did one more trick: Hocus pocus! A change in leadership! From that day on, Mayor Shirley and Treasurer Beulah Boxer led Arlington with kindness and honesty. And of course, they continued the no cats policy.

(PD note: This PD Fairy Tail is based on "The Pied Piper of Hamelin," a very old German story that was popularized by the Brothers Grimm. Moralists say the tale teaches the consequences of greed and the importance of honesty and fulfilling one's promises. But that's ridiculous. Obviously, the moral of the story is No Cats. Ever. Anywhere. Or . . . okay, maybe just that dogs that chase cats should not be scolded but rather rewarded. Preferably with bully sticks.)

Chapter Three

PUG-OCCHIO

𝔖𝔬𝔪𝔢 𝔗𝔦𝔪𝔢 𝔄𝔤𝔬 in a townhouse in Arlington, there lived a sweet toymaker named Mommy who carved a wooden black pug puppet she named PD. Mommy loved her little puppet like she would her own son. She took pug puppet PD everywhere she went: the grocery store, the library, church, the mall, even—to the oft-observed annoyance of both buds and beaus—out on social engagements.

While Mommy adored her pug puppet, she desperately longed for him to be a real dog. She imagined playing with him, walking him, feeding him, and loving him even more, were that possible.

One evening, as Mommy cradled pug puppet PD in her lap while watching day turn to night, she saw a huge, bright star appear in the darkening sky. This luminous heavenly orb seemed to call to her. Mommy was so certain that this star had appeared just for her that she made a wish upon it:

"I wish pug puppet PD could be a real pug," she whispered.

Mommy felt a bit silly—but a bit hopeful, too—as she tucked the pug puppet into its toy bed and hit the hay herself.

Unbeknownst to Mommy, a Lilliputian but big-hearted genie named Janelle heard her wish. Late that night as Mommy dreamt of a life with a living, breathing PD, Janelle the Genie floated into the large, toy-filled room that housed the pug puppet PD's bed and blew magic dust into the puppet, bringing it (now "him") to life. He could move and blink and even think a little, but he remained a puppet pug and not a truly real pug.

Janelle the Genie told PD: "If you prove yourself to be courageous, honest, and unselfish, I will complete your transformation and make you a real live pug."

To help prevent Mommy from going into shock upon discovering this miraculous event, Janelle the Genie conjured up a pad and pencil, jotted a note explaining the situation, and left it next to PD's bed.

Just as she was about to fly back to Genie Land, Janelle the Genie spied a lovely, lively-looking labradoodle peeking into puppet PD's bedroom window. By the surprised look on the little dog's face, Genie Janelle could only assume the labradoodle had witnessed PD's animation. As she stared into the visiting dog's dark eyes—which were as wide as eyes that just witnessed a miracle would be—it occurred to Janelle the Genie that someone would need to keep watch over PD and report to her about his progress in proving himself worthy of becoming a real pug. The already-shocked labradoodle nearly fell over when suddenly Janelle the Genie magically appeared outside the bedroom next to her.

"I'm Janelle," the genie said. "I know you saw me work my magic, and now I need to ask you a favor, Miss . . . ?"

The stunned dog replied, "Yes, um, I'm Lucy the Labradoodle. Please forgive me; I didn't mean to intrude, but I saw lots of sparkles and twinkles coming from this window and . . . well, I'm sorry if I peeked in on something I shouldn't have!"

"No, no," Janelle the Genie replied with a kind smile. "Not only is it okay, but I'm actually glad you're here. As you're now aware, little PD the toy pug puppet has magically become PD the live pug puppet. Still a puppet, but living and breathing, just like you and me."

"I don't quite understand," Lucy the Labradoodle replied. "Please tell me what you think I can offer you and your magic puppet dog."

Janelle the Genie looked from Lucy to PD and back again. "Well, Lucy, I told PD that in order to become a real live dog like you, he has to show some very noble characteristics that prove to me he is worthy of being a real pug.

"Specifically, PD has to live in such a way that makes clear to all onlookers that he is courageous, honest and unselfish. And as the living puppet ventures out into the world and faces new experiences and maybe some trials and temptations, he needs a conscience, Lucy. And I assign you.

"So keep an eye on him and encourage him in the right way to live, okay? And I'll be back someday soon."

And with that, Janelle the Genie flew off, magic dust swirling about her as she went.

Lucy the Labradoodle pranced home, excited to return in the morning to begin her job observing the puppet pug and hopefully helping it to be courageous, honest and unselfish so that the genie would make him a real dog like her.

Meanwhile, inside the home of pug puppet PD, all the commotion down in the toy room had roused Mommy from her slumber. As she entered the room, she couldn't believe her Mommy eyes. PD! Alive! Mommy was overjoyed to read the mysterious note and learn that PD was now a live puppet and—hopefully—on his way to becoming a real dog.

Now that PD was a living puppet, Mommy could take him on real walks. So, that very morning, Mommy and PD set out on their very first walk. Lucy the Labradoodle followed at a distance to keep an eye on PD.

As they ambled along, PD saw a group of dogs and cats laughing and clowning around. Desperate to fit in and make friends, pug puppet PD broke free of his restraint and ran to join them. Two of the pack—con artist Ralph the Dog and his sidekick, Cruella the Cat—gave this strange living, breathing puppet the once-over and then exchanged quick, sneaky, sneery winks.

"Hey there, puppet dog," said the hustler hound with a smirk. "I see by your dog tag that your name is PD the Pug. I'm Ralph the Dog. My feline friend here is Cruella the Cat. We were just about to head to the super fun Stromboli Puppet Show. Why don't you come along? It'll be great!"

Despite the protestations of Lucy the Labradoodle—who had been listening skeptically as the trickster and his tabby tagalong tried to steer PD toward this Stromboli puppeteer person, PD ignored the frantically yelling Mommy and raced off with his newfound alleged pals.

A week passed. Lucy the Labradoodle—who could only imagine what *non*-honorable, *non*-righteous and *non*-honest shenanigans her charge, PD, was up to—and a very melancholy Mommy sat together on Mommy's front porch, staring morosely off into the distance, willing little pug puppet PD to come home.

"Oh dear, oh dear," Mommy fretted, wrapping her arms around herself and rocking back and forth, conveying her distress and discombobulation. "Little labradoodle," she wailed, "where has my PD *gone?* Where could he *be?* What can I *do?*"

It is I who should be doing something, Lucy the Labradoodle wondered worriedly. *Janelle the Genie entrusted me with PD's care, to be PD's conscience, to help him gain moral integrity and thereby become a real dog and not just a living puppet dog. How can I do my job for the genie if I don't even know where pug puppet PD is?*

And as the burden of this great responsibility weighed on her little dog shoulders, Lucy the Labradoodle gave a surprised Mommy a big face lick of encouragement before suddenly bolting from the porch and racing away to try and find PD.

Meanwhile, at Stromboli's Puppet Extravaganza, Mr. Stromboli—who had happily handed hooligans Ralph the

Dog and Cruella the Cat one toy each in exchange for his now top attraction—was making more money than ever, thanks to the crowds coming to see the world's only living, breathing puppet.

Poor, poor PD. Only a week into his miraculous animation, he found himself alone, missing Mommy desperately, and feeling very scared. He stared through the bars of the bird cage that now was his home, through which paying gazers gaped and gawked at this bizarre spectacle: A Real Live Dog Puppet! And, for the umpteenth time since his capture, PD felt real live wet tears falling down his furry face.

Will no one help me? thought pug puppet PD as he nuzzled his nose into the threadbare blanket the stingy Stromboli had laid on the floor of the cage. *How will I escape this horrible puppet circus? How could those meanies Ralph the Dog and Cruella the Cat have done this to me?*

Just then, as if his heart plea had reached Heaven itself, there appeared Janelle the Genie, the very magical being who had brought PD to life just a week prior. PD was very surprised to see her and even more surprised to see a little labradoodle alongside her.

"PD," exclaimed Lucy the Labradoodle, "your Mommy and I have been worried sick. I've been searching and searching for you. Just as I was about to give up, I prayed for a miracle, and *poof!* Janelle the Genie appeared at my side. And the next thing I knew, we were here!

"What happened, PD? How did you end up in a bird cage at the puppet expo?"

Puppet pug PD swallowed hard. He looked at Janelle the Genie, who was watching the two dogs with a sly smile on her elfin face and waiting for PD's explanation. As he was about to admit to having been bamboozled by faux friends who sold him for a couple of lousy toys, he was hit by a strange new emotion: Pride.

Think, PD, think! puppet pug PD demanded of his newly-able-to-reason dog brain. *No way am I going to admit I've been deceived! Duped! Deluded! Not a chance!*

Unable to muster up the courage to be honest, he tried to sound generous, at least. "Well, you see," PD said, staring at the worn, holey fabric under his forepaws, "um, I wanted to buy Mommy some presents, and, um, I read an advertisement seeking living puppets to work for, um, just a week, and then you get money and presents for your Mommy, and, um, then everyone is happy, see?"

Janelle the Genie's bright blue eyes looked from PD to Lucy and back again. "PD," she asked, "would you say Lucy and I and, most importantly, your scared, crying Mommy are—as you put it—'happy'?"

Think, PD!! the now panicking puppet pug pleaded with his brain, pacing his teeny cage. *Make her think you are courageous!*

"Well, of course! Everyone is! Because, see . . ." But before the prevaricating pug puppet could finish his sentence, Janelle the Genie waggled her wand, and suddenly PD's curly pug tail grew ten inches, curling round and round atop his haunches.

"I'm sorry! I'm sorry," the frightened dog sobbed. "Please help me, Janelle the Genie!"

"PD, did I not tell you that, in order to become a real dog, you must be honest, courageous, and unselfish?" Holding her wand above her head, she added, "PD, you've *lied* to Lucy and me. You've *uncourageously* allowed bad animals to lead you astray. And you've *selfishly* left your Mommy to wonder and worry about your wellbeing. You've failed all three tests.

"I am going to free you from your cage and restore your tail to its normal length. But after that, I can offer you no more help. You will be on your own." And with that, a cloud of pixie dust filled the room.

When the dust cleared, PD was outside the puppet expo, all alone. Janelle the Genie and Lucy the Labradoodle had disappeared—hopefully, PD prayed, to tell Mommy he was safe. Well, not safe, but not locked up at least.

And then, into the world that was so very strange to him, ventured a depressed pug puppet PD.

I've ruined everything, he pouted. *Now I'll never be a real dog. I'm forever going to be this oddity, a wooden dog with awkward wooden forelegs and wooden hind legs and a wooden head and body!*

Sullenly sulking as he ambled along, PD was so focused on his pity party—*Oddity! Weirdo! Abnormal! Stiff! Clumsy! Ungraceful! Uncoordinated! Gawky!*—that he didn't notice the sky was rapidly fading from daytime blue to the black of night.

So distracted was the pug puppet that he stumbled right over the small tree branch a sniggering Cruella the Cat had stuck in his path at the direction of that scoundrel Ralph the Dog—the very trickster who'd sold him to the evil puppet master Stromboli. By the time PD got his bearings and clumsily rose to his feet, the cruel pair, joined by several other mean mongrels, encircled him.

"Well, well, well," Ralph the Dog smirked. "Look what we have here. It's PD the puppet! Good timing, puppet dog. I don't know how you escaped Stromboli, but turns out it's a good thing you did!"

Leaning in and staring into the puppet's wooden but very seeing eyes, the devious dog said, "Listen, PD, I know we didn't get off on the right paw, but here's the deal. I got a new job working for a super great human they call the Coachman. I'm paid to find him worthy dogs—like, say, you—and he gives them a ride in his coach to a place called Toy Land.

"It's the best place ever, puppet pug! All the dog toys you could ever play with! All free! What do you say, um, friend?"

The tiny bit of integrity PD had gained from his short time with his conscience Lucy the Labradoodle nagged at his brain. Yet PD couldn't resist the lure of free toys and unlimited playtime. *What dog could?* he reasoned. *Surely this Ralph character isn't so bad. No baddie would bring you to a human who is offering to take you to a place with free playthings, after all!*

"I'm in!" PD exclaimed to the faux friend feigning to be his best bud. "I'm all the way in!"

Before his wooden googly eyes could blink, PD found himself in a large coach alongside a cigarette-smoking

Dalmatian who gave PD a squinty-eyed stare through the haze of smoke surrounding him. "Hey, puppet dog, I'm Dexter the Dalmatian. Where did the Coachman's recruiter find you? I was in the dog pool hall with the other mutts who always skip out of dull doggie daycare to find stuff to get up to. When that Ralph the Dog said I could have free toys and no walkies or furniture rules or any of that other dumb dog stuff my bossy human mommy makes me do, I knew I'd hit the lazy loafer lottery.

"How 'bout you, puppet dog?"

"Um, me too!" PD said, puffing out his pug barrel chest. "Er, a pool hall, yeah! With my smoking and very mischief-minded pool hall chums! I'm PD the Pug, by the way."

Dexter the Dalmatian looked over his new friend as he reached into his pack of cigarettes on the seat of the coach box. "Well, you're a bit odd-looking, but you seem okay to me. Here, have a smoke on me before we get to Toy Land."

PD stared. Again, the bit of morality he'd gleaned from his short moments with his conscience Lucy hounded his head, but only briefly. In and out went thoughts of her admonishing, *PD, you're lying to him. PD, smoking is bad for you. PD, you're pretending to be someone you're not. PD, what would other dogs looking at you think?* Quickly, they were replaced by more selfish musings: *I'm impressing my new pal! I will look so cool smoking and hopefully joining Dexter's pool hall gang! I'm about to get more toys to play with than most any dog in the world! Me! Me! Me! Fun! Fun! Fun!*

"Yo! PD! Snap to!" Dexter the Dalmatian barked, handing him a cigarette he'd lit from the one hanging down from his flews.

This is embarrassing, pug puppet PD thought. *I don't smoke! I don't even know how to smoke! I can't let my only friend know I'm not cool like him!*

Think, PD, think! "Er, I would," PD bluffed with a brash boldness he didn't know he possessed. "But, see . . . I just happen to be taking a special doggie medicine that doesn't work as well if you smoke. So, wow, I'm so bummed I can't right now. Er, normally I would smoke, and other bad stuff, too. Because I am very cool and also in a dog gang called, um, the Dog Gang."

Suddenly, PD felt his puppet tail expand, again corkscrewing round and round and round on the area where his bum met his thankfully sturdy back. It spiraled and spiraled, adding more and more inches to its expanding length, only pausing when the pug puppet hung his head, gulped and confessed:

"Okay! Okay! That's not true! But I don't really want to smoke right now, if that's all right with you, Dexter."

The nonplussed Dalmatian watched PD's tail as its bizarre growth spurt ended, then gave pug puppet PD a perplexed peer before shaking his broad head and putting the offered lit butt next to the one he already was enjoying. "Whatever you say, weirdo wood dog," he uttered between the two smokes. "More for me.

"Plus, there's Toy Land just up ahead, so it's time to put the cigs away and get excited! I hope it's as great as Ralph the Dog promised me it'd be. 'Toys galore!' he said. 'Zero work!' he said. 'Endless fun!' he said. I can't wait!"

And PD—despite the teensy, weensy warning he imagined Janelle the Genie whispering in his button ear—couldn't help but get caught up in Dexter the Dalmatian's fervor. He wagged his now rather-too-long tail, causing his little pug body to wobble while his round head bobbled in excited anticipation. As the Coachman shook the reins of the team of horses driving them to the so-called enchanted play land, both dogs in his charge had the same thought: *Toys and joys—what could possibly go wrong?*

Meanwhile, back at Mommy's toy shop, it was all Mommy could do to create even one toy a day. "Who cares?" she sobbed quietly as she spent most of the day staring out the window—certainly allocating more time to staring than to plying her craft. "Who cares about fulfilling toy orders when the only one I care about—my living toy, PD—is out who-knows-where, meeting who-knows-who, doing who-knows-what?"

The labradoodle at her feet desperately wished she could speak human. She could have answered all three of Mommy's queries, having learned all about Ralph the Dog, Cruella the Cat, and the tricksters' tricks that lured pug puppet PD to the wicked Stromboli. And while Lucy the Labradoodle could only guess what might be happening in the days since she and Janelle the Genie disappeared from PD's side, leaving him to find his own way, the labradoodle feared he was unequipped to handle the many temptations dangled by con artists like Ralph the Dog.

Back in the Coachman's carriage, an anxious pair of dogs were bouncing on their cushy seats, excitedly whipping their heads back and forth from one window to the other as the Coachman announced they were arriving at their destination.

"There it is, Dexter!" PD exclaimed, pointing at the gigantic *Welcome to Toy Land* billboard that proclaimed that their holiday away from home would be *Fun! Fun! Fun!* with *No Rules! No Mommies and Daddies!* and *Nothing But Toys & Freedom!* "This is going to be great!"

As the carriage came to a stop, pug puppet PD and Dexter the Dalmatian hopped out of the coach box and raced to the Toy Land entrance, wagging their tails at the silently cackling Coachman who was turning his carriage around, no doubt to collect the next Toy Land "customer" duped by his lackey Ralph the Dog.

"No rules, PD! No authority!" Dexter the Dalmatian whooped as the pair entered what appeared to be a park created from a bad boy's wish list. "Look, PD! There's so much fun awaiting us!"

Pug puppet PD thought he was dreaming. Any guilt over the fear he more than likely was causing Mommy and that so-called conscience labradoodle dog quickly evaporated as he read the dozen or so signs posted before each "land" within Toy Land:

Toys Galore Land!

Pool Hall Land!

Smokers' and Drinkers' Land!

Gambling Land!

Fighting Land!

Graffiti Lesson Land!

On it went, one fun spot after the other. PD and Dexter hardly knew where to begin. Within hours, they had engaged in more debauchery than PD had previously known existed: smoking, fighting, vandalizing, drinking (nonalcoholic dog beer), playing pool, and other shenanigans.

For a full week, it was all fun, no rules, no responsibilities. Despite an occasional tug at his heart for Mommy, pug puppet PD thought this was the "good" life he deserved. He had more playthings than ever before, and more friendships—albeit not like the friendships between humans and dogs he had witnessed during his time with Mommy and on his first walk. It was *great, great, great!*

Until it wasn't.

Unbeknownst to poor PD and poor Dexter the Dalmatian and their poor alleged pals, Toy Land hid a curse that affected all "guests": after the first week, everyone was transformed into cats, after which they were sold by the Coachman to the government of Cat Island in faraway Japan to live out their days entertaining tourists. And for puppet pug PD and Dexter the Dalmatian, transformation time had come.

A terrified PD watched Dexter turn from Dalmatian to calico cat and get thrown in the Coachman's coach. As he sensed the start of a similar change in himself, he looked up to see a miracle: Lucy the Labradoodle was racing toward him holding a huge net. Seconds later, PD found himself ensnared in its mesh and being hurriedly dragged out of Toy Land by his huffing and puffing rescuer. Alas, while he and Lucy managed to flee before his transformation was complete, PD did have a cat's ears, whiskers and tail.

"You're lucky I found you. I overheard that rascally Ralph the Dog boasting to his buds about his new job taking gullible dogs to some Coachman person who bought them here," Lucy the Labradoodle said as she and the now running-on-his own PD hustled toward Mommy's house. "It took a while to find that domain of depravity, but at least I got there before you were sold to Cat World, like your friend I saw in the Coachman's carriage."

They raced the rest of the way to Mommy's, PD's face going from terrified to gleeful as his happy home came into view. But as the two dogs—well, one dog and one part-dog, part-cat puppet—entered, they found her toy shop deserted. As they frantically looked around, some pixie dust swirled around the room and a letter from Janelle the Genie appeared in Lucy the Labradoodle's paws.

"Oh no, PD!" Lucy the Labradoodle cried. "Janelle the Genie says your Mommy followed me to Toy Land, but on the way there she was abducted by Stromboli, who put her in his cage, saying he'd trade her freedom for your return as his star attraction! Oh this is awful, just awful!

"PD!" scolded Lucy. The pug puppet's hired conscience looked up from the paper in her paws and shook her head, a disappointed look on her furry face. "Why couldn't you have just listened to Janelle the Genie and been courageous and honest and unselfish?

"Gosh, PD! Why couldn't you have just been *good?*"

As reality hit—as PD stared at his cat tail and took in his pool hall body odor and looked at his nicotine-stained paws and smelled his own sour nonalcoholic doggie beer breath—he knew he was the reason Mommy was now in a cage. The same cage he himself had been trapped within just a few weeks prior.

It might be too late for me to earn the blessing from Janelle the Genie and become a real dog, PD thought, *but it isn't too late for me to rescue Mommy and get her home and at least be her good little living pug puppet from now on.*

And with that thought, pug puppet PD tore off, with a shocked Lucy the Labradoodle dashing after him. As they sneaked onto the Puppet Show fairgrounds, Lucy was about to remind her charge to try and tread quietly on his wooden (now cat) paws. Alas, his clumsy stiff forelegs tripped over another puppet on the ground outside the tent with the cage they knew was holding PD's Mommy. His wooden head smacked into a ticket booth serving paying customers, the noise attracting stares from those nearest them . . .

Including the last three beings PD and Lucy the Labradoodle hoped to run into: Stromboli and his minions Ralph the Dog and Cruella the Cat.

"Well, Ralph, looks like I didn't waste those toys on you and your sidekick here after all," Stromboli grunted, leaning to leer at the half-dog, half-cat puppet oddity at his feet. "I guess my star attraction is back from the Toy Land adventure you sent him on. And, judging by the goofy looks of him, I'd say he escaped just in time to avoid being sold by the Coachman to Cat World. The Coachman's loss is my gain. Between that whining, wailing, weeping woman in the cage now and this freaky puppet, Stromboli's Puppet Show will be the most talked-about extravaganza on Earth!"

Whipping his head around to Ralph the Dog, Stromboli then roared, "Grab him, Ralph! Toss him in with that weepy woman. We can double the ticket price!" Turning to the real feline, he yelled, "Cruella! Go make a sign to post outside: *The Bawling Beauty and her Half-Dog, Half-Cat.*

As pug puppet PD was thrown in the cage with his Mommy— whose expression changed from grief to grin when she saw her PD next to her, and then to fear at the realization they now were trapped together—Lucy ran to find Janelle the Genie. But PD knew they couldn't know if the fairy would be found in time. He had to act.

I caused all this, he thought. *I want my final act to be one of courage, honesty and unselfishness.*

With all his little pug puppet might, PD then beat his wooden body over and over again against the cage's locked door. It took a good one hundred hard smacks, but finally the lock gave way and the door flew open, to the sheer shock of puppeteer Stromboli and his two lackeys, who certainly were unprepared for this turn of events.

With the tiny amount of puppet life left in his broken body, the puppet pug pushed Mommy as hard as he could, willing her to run. His last view out of his wooden googly eyes before expiring was a crying Mommy racing past Stromboli, knocking over the paying crowd gathered to see this spectacle—who doubtless would be seeking refunds—and disappearing into distance.

As PD was tossed into the fire pit to be burned with other used-up puppets, now just another inanimate toy, there suddenly appeared all around the hot furnace a beautiful sparkling light. And amazingly, PD's little body rose from the flames, his miraculously unburned body slowly landing in the lawn nearby.

"Welcome back, courageous, honest, unselfish little PD," Janelle the Genie sang over him. "You have proven yourself worthy to be a real live pug. Now," the fairy said, hugging the weeping, no-longer-wooden, wonderfully soft little bundle of love, "let's get you home where you belong. Home with your Mommy and Lucy and all the happiness coming your way. You've earned it."

(PD note: This PD Fairy Tail is based on The Adventures of Pinocchio *by Carlo Collodi. The story has many morals. We're supposed to learn that disobedience is bad, that lying is bad, that being a chicken-liver 'fraidy-cat is bad. That's nice and all, but I think it's more about pushing Mommy to the absolute limit—like doing what I want when I want how I want and getting into all sorts of no-no shenanigans—right up to that point where she gives me the stink-eye and takes my bully stick away. And* that *is when you switch over to good dog! And act righteous and obedient! To get your treat back! And to not go in a bird cage, er, your crate, for a time out.)*

Chapter Four

THE THREE LITTLE PUGS

𝕭𝖆𝖈𝖐 𝕴𝖓 𝖄𝖊𝖘𝖙𝖊𝖗𝖞𝖊𝖆𝖗 there lived three little pugs.

There was Needy Pug, an anxious, antsy, jumpy, jittery, unsettled, unsure, pestered, perturbed pug.

There was Seedy Pug, a dishonorable, despicable, sleazy, sloppy, noxious, nasty, petty, plotting pug.

And there was PD Pug, a rational, reasonable, steady, strategic, conscientious, committed, prudent, practical pug.

Although possessing very different dispositions, the three little pugs were palsy pals who roughhoused and rollicked and reveled whenever they were together.

Of course they were not always together due to their contrasting conduct. Needy Pug spent his idle hours all a-twitter and a-jitter; Seedy Pug literally gambled his spare time away, rolling the dice and getting into vice. Only PD Pug made

the most of each day, being industrious and showing ingenuity and integrity every day and in every way.

One day, the three pugs decided they were of age to move
out of their mommies' and daddies' homes and build their
own doghouses.

Needy Pug immediately worked out in his brain that he
had never worked out in his body so it would be unwise to
overly tax his puny muscles. He figured that straw would
make a fine fortress, a restful refuge, at least some phys-
ical fencing between him and whichever bogeyman was
bewitching his mind at the moment. His straw structure
brought a scarcely seen skip in his step; he felt safe within
the dry stalk construction.

Seedy Pug had more brawn than his buddy but also a non-
existent love of labor, due to a preference for gin joints
and gaining gambling points. He stealthily stole twigs from
nearby neighbors' kindling collections and soon created a
bungalow from these branchlets. He took pride in the pid-
dling effort that went into his home production and then
rewarded himself with what he decided was well-deserved
debauchery, heading off to scam some sucker in the shell
game he often led at the park.

PD Pug, meanwhile, took much longer to complete his home
than his friends. He labored over available land, checking
on topography, topsoil, water and gas, power and grass, zone
laws, bone laws, and tax and other facts. After buying a nice
flat plot, PD Pug hired an architect who did a blueprint, a
structural engineer who advised him on specifications and

safety protocols, and a title company specialist who verified there were no liens on PD Pug's chosen property.

Following this responsible research, practical PD Pug decided on his building material choice. He opted for brick, known for its sustainability, energy efficiency, durability, and sturdiness. Off he went to Home Depot, the twenty-percent-off coupon he'd torn from the newspaper he peed on that morning securely tucked in his collar.

A week later, PD Pug had built a brick home so expertly constructed that it was named Doghouse of the Year by the editors of *DogHouse Beautiful Magazine*. And once he had collected enough gently used cushions, mismatched dishware and other tossed-away home items at the county dump, his home caught the eye of *Elle's Dog Decor Magazine* to boot. PD's brick house was the talk of the dog park!

The only two dogs *not* raving about PD Pug's pad were his pals Needy Pug and Seedy Pug, whose straw and stick homes were not attracting attention even from *Waste Bin Weekly*, published by the local landfill organization.

"PD thinks he's the canine Chip Gaines or something," Needy Pug snorted to Seedy Pug. "My straw house took two days to erect and—other than an occasional draft getting through the little gaps here and there—it's just fine! I wasn't about to worry myself sick stewing over straw structure standards! Who needs all that erection perfection and security silliness? Right, Seedy?"

"Exactly!" Seedy grunted. "My sticks are sturdy enough to keep, well, *most* of the rain out. And, um, the editors of

Teepee Today will be calling any minute now, you watch, you just watch! Plus! PD is so obsessed with doing everything 'just right' all the time. It's a house, not a fortress, for dog's sake!"

Just then, Needy Pug and Seedy Pug looked up to see their friend sniffing around the tiny trees they each had just planted on their properties.

"Oh, hi guys!" PD Pug said, looking up from Seedy Pug's sapling, against which he'd just relieved himself. "I was just noticing how young the trees in both your yards are."

PD Pug paused, pointing a few dog doors down. "You'll note that the tall, sturdy oaks over there at my doghouse are providing a lot more privacy from prying eyes than your baby trees are. They also are saving me a lot on fertilizer and other early tree-need costs and already are upping my property value due to the enhanced beauty they offer my yard.

"Oh! And they help the environment more than yours, because mature trees absorb more carbon and improve air quality better than the newbies. And they withstand drought better since they need less water.

"Yep, you guys shoulda sought land parcels with older trees, like I did," PD Pug proudly added, trotting off to graze his growing lawn.

"He's insufferable!" whispered a now-extra-nervous Needy Pug to a sneering Seedy Pug, who showed his agreement with a googly-eyed eye roll. "But is he *right? Are* we unprotected, Seedy? Should I worry? More, I mean?"

"First, *yes,* PD is being unbearable! And, *no,* you are *not* in any danger of anything, other than almost working too hard!" Seedy Pug puffed. "He can have his magazine interviews and his tall trees and those fancy used pillows and dog bowls he foraged for. Who cares about all this home safety and privacy and blah blah blah?

"I mean, I have my playing cards and dice I swiped from that man's bag when he left the game store; I have the big tray of cookies I snatched off that old woman's window sill, where they were cooling; and you have the chill chews I stole for you from the pharmacy recycling bin. And we have houses, too! Just like PD Pug! We are plenty safe!"

"Um, right," meekly muttered Needy Pug, not seeming convinced his dwelling was as secure as he'd claimed earlier. "I'm sure you're right; all will be fine. I mean, it's not like we live in the woods, Seedy, right?"

The pair of pug pals padded off to their homes of straw and sticks, reminding one another along the way that they lived among dogs, not dinosaurs, and that there were no monsters around, neither in the neighborhood nor under their beds. By the time they parted and entered their straw and stick structures, they were in agreement that that silly PD Pug was simply too practical for his own good!

But the following morning's news programs and periodicals had Needy Pug panicking and Seedy Pug zoning out on dog hemp chews and drinking nonalcoholic dog beers at the pub.

"This just in! This just in!" the host of *Get Up, Dog!* announced at the top of the popular morning show's first hour. "The Big Bad Wolf has been spotted heading toward our town! Officials predict this frightening and danger-ous-to-all-dogs enemy will be in our vicinity by tomorrow morning! City Councilwoman Alicia Akita says officials are urging all dogs to stock up on kibble and water and lock their doghouse doors!"

After grabbing a final lick from the dog beer tap at the tav-ern and swiping the bowl of beer nuts from the bar counter, Seedy Pug exited to find Needy Pug fidgeting and fretting, jigging and jittering. "Seedy!" hollered Needy Pug as his hemped-up playmate pitched forward unsteadily. "We need to get provisions! And then we need to get home! The Big Bad Wolf is coming!"

"Oh please," Seedy Pug slurred before mocking his friend by breaking out in song: "Who's afraid of the Big Bad Wolf, the Big Bad Wolf, the Big Bad Wolf? Tra-la-la-la-la!"

But looking at Needy's fear-filled face, Seedy paused his singing and reached into the stash of chill chews tucked in his collar. "Here, pal, have a chill chew and stop worry-ing! We'll go to the dog food store, then head home to the security of our plenty-secure homes! Nothing to fear! Sing along, Needy!"

Soon the chill chew slowed Needy Pug's racing heart. He began to sing, tentatively at first, but gaining more gaiety and glee as he began trusting Seedy Pug's promise that they needn't fear the Big Bad Wolf.

"Who's afraid of the Big Bad Wolf, the Big Bad Wolf, the Big Bad Wolf? Tra-la-la-la-la!" the cronies crowed, getting louder and drawing the eyes of other dogs who looked at them curiously as they went about their business of preparing for possibly impending peril.

And two of those eyes belonged to their pug buddy PD, who was passing the pub on his way to the dog park water fountain, his sack carrying ten empty water bottles he had collected from area trash cans.

"What on Earth are you two *doing* here?" PD Pug exclaimed, yelling loud enough to be heard over the chorusing couple. "You need to get *food*! You need to get *water*! You need to *get home*! The Big Bad Wolf is coming!"

Seedy Pug, who had sobered up by now, stared at his friend, trying to convey courage. Needy Pug stood tall but looked to Seedy for confidence rather than meeting the goggle from PD's googlies. "Look, PD," Seedy snarled, "why don't you mind your own business? We were *just* on our way to the market. Plus, this allegedly big and bad wolf isn't even due here 'til tomorrow. So lighten up, PD!"

"Um, yeah. What he said," Needy Pug mumbled, keeping his eyes on his forepaws. "We, um, are just fine."

PD Pug nodded his round pug head, looking from one of his pals to the other. "Okay, you two. But please take care. The news said the Big Bad Wolf is very mean and very hungry. Please get your dog food and get home as soon as possible!" And with that, PD Pug was off to the water fountain to get enough water to last several days.

The next morning, all area hounds—including Needy Pug and Seedy Pug, who had at least heeded PD Pug's words enough to speed up their kibble shopping and get home by nightfall—were hunkered down in their locked doghouses. And as *Get Up, Dog!* began broadcasting, the dogs felt dog-gone lucky to be inside.

"The Big Bad Wolf is here! The Big Bad Wolf is here!" anchor dog Amy Airedale announced, an alarmed look on her furry face. "All dogs are advised to stay home until officials deem it safe to go on walkies. For now, use your Pee Pads and await further updates!"

Needy Pug shuddered as he shut off the news and double-checked the locks on his doghouse door and its little window shutters. Ignoring his toys and his bowl of breakfast kibble, he pushed against the panic that was rapidly rising within him. He paced and paced, patrolling the tiny indoor area, telling himself that maybe he should sing, like his playmate Seedy; maybe, he reasoned, that would calm him.

"Who's afraid of the Big Bad Wolf, the Big Bad Wolf, the Big Bad Wolf? Who's afraid of the Big Bad Wolf, the Big Bad Wolf, the Big Bad Wolf?" he sang, getting louder and louder and more self-assured the more he repeated the lyrics. Before long, Needy Pug had channeled Seedy Pug's courage. "Who's afraid of the Big Bad Wolf! Not me, not me! Who's afraid of the Big Bad Wolf? Not me, not me, not me, not me, not . . ."

As he danced about, Needy Pug was singing so loudly that he failed to hear the banging on his little doghouse door until it reached a level that drowned out his ditty. Assuming it was a bored Seedy Pug come to play, Needy Pug was just about to open the doghouse door when the voice on the other size froze him to his spot on the floor.

"Little pug, little pug, let me come in!"

The voice was unmistakably that of a scary wolf. A *big* wolf. A *bad* wolf.

Oh no! Needy Pug thought, his furry little body shaking uncontrollably. *It's not just a big, bad wolf, it is the Big Bad Wolf! He's real and he's here! What to do? What to do?*

More panicked than he'd ever been during any past panic attack, little Needy Pug dug deep for some pug pluckiness, took a big breath from his barrel chest, and called out:

"No! Not by the fur of my furry chin chin!"

"Then I'll huff and I'll puff and I'll blow your doghouse in!" roared the Big Bad Wolf.

Please, straw, be strong! Keep me safe! prayed Needy Pug. Alas, 'twas not to be. Moments later, the little dog heard the Big Bad Wolf inhale a huge amount of air into his huge Big Bad Wolf lungs. The next thing Needy Pug knew, straw was flying all around him as his poorly constructed home broke into pieces and straw was strewn everywhere.

Thankfully, Needy Pug possessed enough presence of mind to process the danger he was in. Shoving off the hay pieces under which he was buried, he powered up his little pug body and sprinted to Seedy Pug's house, with the Big Bad

Wolf not far behind him. He banged on Seedy Pug's door and yelled until his friend finally opened the door just wide enough to grab Needy Pug's collar and yank him inside.

"What happened, Needy?" a surprised Seedy Pug enquired as he quickly relocked the door and spun around to face his friend. "What's wrong? What's gotten into you?"

Needy Pug paused a moment to catch his breath. "Oh, Seedy! He's real! He's real! The Big Bad Wolf came to my house, and he told me to let him in! But I knew he'd eat me, so I said, 'No! Not by the fur of my furry chin chin!' But he blew my straw house down! And he would have eaten me, but I ran here and now I'm safe!"

Seedy Pug, who was mid–nonalcoholic dog beer guzzle when Needy Pug began his narrative, set his bottle down and looked from his doghouse door to his pal and back again.

"Needy! Are you telling me your straw house couldn't keep out a silly wolf? Hmmmph! Hard to believe! It seemed plenty sturdy enough! Well, regardless, you are just fine now. You are welcome to stay here in my very safe stick house for as long as you need. Help yourself to the dog booze and hemp chews. I stole plenty!"

"Gee, thanks, Seedy!" Needy exclaimed, breathing a big sigh of relief. "I feel so much better being here surrounded by these strong sticks!" Sniffing the air, Needy added, "It *is* secure, right, Seedy? I'm getting a bit of a draft coming in through the gaps over here."

Seedy rolled his googly eyes and took a drag on the stub of the hand-rolled cigar he'd found in the gutter outside. "Look, Needy, do you want to stay or not? Obviously, it's secure. I mean, you don't see any Big Bad Wolf trying to blow . . ."

Just then, the very voice Needy Pug had hoped never to hear again bellowed just outside Seedy Pug's pad.

"Little pugs, little pugs, let me come in!" the Big Bad Wolf roared.

A shocked Seedy Pug was rendered mute, so surprised was he by the presence of this menace. He stubbed out his stogie and swigged the rest of the suds and fought his growing fear.

"No!" Seedy Pug bellowed from the pit of his pug belly. "Not by the fur of our furry chin chins!"

"Erm, yeah!" his horrified housemate meekly chimed in. "Yeah! What he said!"

But their words fell on determined-to-get-a-pug-dinner ears.

"Then I'll huff and I'll puff and I'll blow your doghouse in!" thundered the Big Bad Wolf. And a moment later, he was inhaling deeply.

As the scrawny twigs and sprigs crumbled all around them, Needy Pug—knowing he and Seedy were on the wolf's dinner menu—showed a shocking amount of pug plunk and spunk. He grabbed Seedy Pug's collar in his teeth and dragged his pal out the door, not letting go until he'd raced them both straight to PD Pug's place.

"PD! PD! It's us! Open up!" yelled Needy Pug. He swiveled his thick pug neck back and saw the Big Bad Wolf bearing down on them. Desperately, the little dog yelled again—PD! PD! PD!" as he and Seedy banged on the door.

Moments later, a big googly eyeball was peering through the peephole in PD Pug's doghouse door.

"Who is it?" PD calmly queried. "I'm not about to open my door when there's danger lurking about."

"It's us!! Needy and Seedy! Let us in!" Seedy Pug pleaded. "The Big Bad Wolf blew both our doghouses in! He wants to eat us, but we escaped and ran here! Please, PD! Help us, PD!"

Seedy and Needy heard numerous clicks and clacks as PD opened his security locks and tapped in the code to turn off the security alarm. Finally, just as the Big Bad Wolf was about to snatch them in his jaws, the door cracked open, the frightened friends slipped inside, and PD slammed his door shut and reactivated the locks.

Pounding on the thick wood door that stood strong between him and the doggie dinner he desired, the Big Bad Wolf blustered his by-now-known demand:

"Little pugs, little pugs, let me in!"

A much shakier than normal Needy Pug, a now very sobered-up Seedy Pug, and a justifiably scared but entirely focused-on-forming-a-plan PD Pug stood three abreast in the middle of the room, their paws nervously kneading the warm rug PD Pug had found curbside outside a nice home on a recent trash day.

"Okay, my pug compadres, here's the deal." PD looked from Needy Pug to Seedy Pug as he began to lay out his plan on how to avoid becoming the Big Bad Wolf's three-dog lunch. "I am very confident my sturdy brick house will withstand the Big Bad Wolf's attempt to get in.

"We need to portray pug imperturbability. We will show this Big Bad Wolf that he has met his match! We will be cool, calm, and composed! We will exude self-possession, self-control, self-assurance! Try as he might, he won't be able to get to us. My home will keep us safe."

While Needy Pug unconvincingly gave a little nod of his noggin, Seedy Pug stared at his pug pal with incredulity.

"Are you cat-brained?" Seedy Pug cried, beginning to pace the length of PD Pug's doghouse. "You're so smart normally! This wolf wants to eat us!! He almost ate me and Needy!! We are done for!!"

Outside the doghouse, the demand was roared again:

"Little pugs, little pugs, let me in!"

Looking around at his excellently-constructed home and thinking of the secure, durable bonding between the bricks thanks to the high-quality mortar he'd chosen, the metal ties that held the bricks tightly in place; the waterproofing material he'd been sure to place behind the bricks, and his home's ability to withstand winds up to 185 miles per hour, PD Pug told his friends:

"That Big Bad Wolf ain't getting in, guys."

Meanwhile, the Big Bad Wolf, who was not privy to all this talk over this allegedly safe and solid structure, was thinking of one thing: pug lunch. Pacing in anger over having been ignored, he yelled out one more time: "Little pugs, little pugs, let me in!"

"Not by the fur of our furry chin chins!" PD Pug yelled back. Amazingly, he wore a slight grin on his wide, flat pug face, unlike Needy Pug and Seedy Pug, both of whom looked terrified since they remained convinced they soon would be in the belly of their tormentor.

"Then I'll huff and I'll puff and I'll blow your doghouse in!" the Big Bad Wolf hollered.

Moments later, the trio heard the Big Bad Wolf take a huge breath. And then they heard him blow with all his Big Bad Wolf might. And then . . .

Nothing.

PD's house stood. Not a single brick shifted.

But his pals remained sure of their coming bad fate. "How much longer do you think we have, Seedy?" whispered Needy Pug tremulously. "How much longer 'til the Big Bad Wolf eats us? Do you think we have time to pray for our sins? I want to go to Dog Heaven, Seedy! I'm *scared*, Seedy!!"

Seedy Pug stared into his friend's wider-than-usual googly eyes. "All the time in the world ain't enough time for me to get forgiveness. I'm a goner. But I will pray and hope.

"And I could use a smoke right about now, that's for sure. I'm scared too, Needy."

The Big Bad Wolf pounded on the solid wood door and shrieked and demanded to be admitted. He blew and blew, over and over, without success. Finally, he headed to the doghouse roof, where PD had built a little chimney. All the while, PD continued feeling and acting calm.

"Stop it, you two," said PD to his fearful friends. "First, God forgives even dogs like you, Seedy. But you're not going to be anybody's lunch. I have a plan. Let's turn the tables on that Big Bad Wolf!"

PD Pug then raced to the kitchen and got a big pot and filled it with water. As Needy Pug and Seedy Pug stared at one another in confusion, PD lit a flame on the stove and watched the water quickly come to a boil. Then he grabbed the mismatched quilted potholders he'd found outside the town's Goodwill, carried the hot pot to the fireplace, and set it on the grate in the firebox. And then PD Pug threw in a cup of turpentine.

The three little pugs waited. And waited. And waited. And then . . .

Right on cue, the Big Bad Wolf—visions of Pug Pie in his big bad brain—sucked in his big bad gut, slid down the chimney, and got a very big and very bad surprise.

"Yeeeeee-ouch!" he screamed as he landed in the scalding-hot pot. As the Big Bad Wolf splashed about, the turpentine PD had added met the flames and ignited, once again demonstrating the practicality and ingenuity of the well-read, well-educated pug. The Big Bad Wolf, his fur now aflame, ran shrieking out the door, down the road, and all the way to the town lake, where he dived in. His racing heart slowed, and he felt relief. But only for a moment.

"You! Come out with your paws up!"

On the shore of the lake, surrounded by the no-longer-shaking Needy Pug and Seedy Pug and the chiller-than-ever PD Pug, stood city councilwoman Alicia Akita. The leader yelled through a bullhorn raised to her broad, massive head. "Out! Now! The police are the way. You will be charged with terrorizing dogs throughout the city!

"You are a *very* bad wolf! A Big Bad Wolf!"

As the police led the Big Bad Wolf away, the councilwoman proclaimed PD Pug a town hero and placed the town's coveted *Most Practical Citizen* medal around his neck.

PD Pug beamed at his pals Needy Pug and Seedy Pug. "Okay, guys," PD Pug said to his finally smiling chums, "let's go build a couple more *brick* doghouses!"

(PD note: This PD Fairy Tail is based on "The Three Little Pigs" by Joseph Jacobs. The fabulist people say the lesson here is that preparation is necessary for success, shortcuts can have major consequences, and hard work pays off. What is with these moralists getting it so wrong all the time? Clearly the moral of this tale is that when danger is coming, Mommy needs to get to the grocery store before the shelves are picked over and then she comes home with icky generic dog food and generic milk bones that aren't real Milk Bone brand milk bones. Which has happened. And I didn't appreciate it, either.)

Chapter Five

PRINCE PD AND THE PAUPER

Once There Lived in the tiny village of Borsum a poor black pug named Googly. He lived in the tiny home of his sweet but impoverished Great Auntie Sheila, who adopted little Googly as her own after she saw him searching for food scraps near the town dumpster.

She named him Googly, both because he became so very wide-eyed whenever he saw food and because his huge orbs reminded her of the drawings of hungry, needy waifs depicted in the popular paintings of Margaret Keane.

Although she couldn't offer Googly nice things like sequined dog collars, premium dog food, or a climate-controlled doghouse with wool carpet, Great Auntie Sheila could offer Googly things money can't buy: lots of cuddles, lots of walkies, and lots of love and happiness.

Great Auntie Sheila did not have the means to enroll little Googly in the expensive dog training lessons afforded by the parents of his dog pals. But Googly was able to learn plenty of obedience-school skills just by mimicking other dogs out on walkies and on the dog television shows he sometimes watched on their tiny black and white television. By the time he was six, Googly had the manners and mannerisms of the dogs owned by the village's wealthiest humans. Great Auntie Sheila was so proud of Googly; she stood so tall when walking him around the village square and seeing how he acted so much classier than she could ever have imagined when she found him scavenging just a few short years before.

As hard as it would have been for Googly to believe, there were places in the world where foraging for food was a foreign concept. There were places where the humans didn't need to count their pennies and wonder if they would be able to pay the rent that month. There were places where the only worry was whether the weather would cooperate with that day's fun plans.

And the best example of this type of place was located on the outskirts of Borsum, just a half-hour's doggie walkie away from Great Auntie Sheila's home. It was the grand and magnificent and opulent and majestic Mommy Royale, the Royal Palace of the region's ruler, Queen Mommy. Beautiful and kind Queen Mommy ruled her queendom with a satin glove, treating all with benevolence and compassion. She focused on the welfare of her subjects in Borsum and the many other villages in her realm. Queen Mommy was known by all for her generosity of spirit, her sunny disposition, and her ability to bring joy and happiness wherever she went.

But nowhere and to no one did Queen Mommy demonstrate the level of adoration, affection, devotion, kindness and concern as she did to the love of her life: her little black pug, PD.

Queen Mommy loved dogs. Before choosing one, she had read a great deal about various dog breeds. She learned that pugs were originally bred in China as companions for royalty and other wealthy citizens. Highly valued by Chinese emperors, the breed was treated regally, living lives of luxury with guards and servants. Some pugs were even given titles and ranks.

So Queen Mommy decided to adopt a pug, and she chose PD from a litter at the best kennel in Borsum.

Queen Mommy knew that a breed with royal bloodlines was the perfect companion for a queen. So she felt it only right and just that her little PD be named Prince of Mommy Royale. For his official coronation ceremony, Queen Mommy brought in religious leaders who anointed PD with holy oil and administered an oath to help Mommy rule justly, to which PD dutifully barked his loyalty (or so Queen Mommy assumed, anyway). Prince PD was even given his own doggie-sized crown, scepter and orb.

While she was aware that Queen Victoria of Great Britain had owned thirty-eight pugs, Queen Mommy was more than happy focusing all her love on her little Prince PD. When she wasn't busy with her queenly duties, she was always with Prince PD, feeding him, playing with him, walking him, and cuddling with him—unless, of course, he was off playing with his dog friends or just romping about in the palatial gardens, marking the trees, chasing squirrels, and giving the gardeners plenty of work by digging up flowers and burying bones . . .

. . . and, occasionally, sneaking off the Mommy Royale grounds to sniff around the area villages. As Prince PD matured, he grew more and more curious about life beyond the palace walls.

What do the doggies in the villages do every day? pondered Prince PD, who was now six years old. *Do they enjoy as much amusement and pleasure as I do with Mommy and my PD pals in our palace land? I'll bet they would be excited to meet a real prince and frolic and frisk and romp and revel with me! After my Royal Nap, I think I'll go sniff around the neighboring villages and see if I can find some new fun friends!*

Meanwhile, one of those village dogs was wondering a similar thing. Back in Borsum, little Googly was gazing out the window at the pretty skies and wishing he was outside on a walkie meeting friends instead of being cooped up inside their little cottage. So, as Great Auntie Sheila napped, Googly quietly slipped through his old wooden dog door, and off he went into the neighborhood.

Googly couldn't decide whether to go on a wee-wee marking tour of the area or maybe visit the local dog park to hang with his buds, or—*No!* Today he would use his free time to venture out of his locality and see what was beyond the village of Borsum. And off he went!

A couple hours later, back at the palace, Prince PD had completed his Royal Nap, during which he dreamed of that trek through the villages he had pondered partaking in earlier.

He checked that Queen Mommy was engrossed in her Royal Reading, then went through his Royal Doggy Door and raced away.

But as Prince PD bounded down the beautiful flower-lined path away from the palace, he noticed another dog—a black pug, like himself—loitering around the Mommy Royale gates. He saw that this pug, in his excitement over the beauty and majesty he was beholding, wandered a bit too close to the palace gate, drawing the attention of the always-on-high-alert palace guards, who grabbed the startled dog and withdrew their batons to beat him for possibly posing a threat to Queen Mommy's well-being.

Pumping his little pug legs, Prince PD scurried to the gates to prevent the punishing of the visiting dog. Pretending to know him and to have been awaiting his arrival, Prince PD put his paw on the newcomer. "Welcome, friend!" said PD as he wagged his curled tail at the palace guards, causing them to unhand the shaking, shabby-looking visitor. The next thing Googly knew, Prince PD was ushering him through the gates and into his chamber within the palace.

There in Prince PD's Royal Bedroom, the two dogs spent hours getting to know one another, each fascinated by the other's life.

They also were completely astounded by how alike they looked. The resemblance was uncanny. As the hours went by and life stories continued to be shared, they learned, amazingly, that they had been born not only on the same day but at the same Borsum kennel and in the same litter!

And that gave Prince PD an idea for what he thought was a comical caper, a great gag to pull on Queen Mommy.

"So, Googly, what do you think of this bright idea I just brainstormed?" posed Prince PD to his new friend. "How about we trade places? For the next month, I'll live in the village of Borsum with your Great Auntie Sheila, and you'll live here at Mommy Royale with my Mommy, or, as you know her, Queen Mommy. How funny would that be?"

"Oh, I love it!" Googly giggled, nodding his broad head in excitement. "But how would we pull it off? I mean, surely the Queen Mommy and my Great Auntie Sheila would quickly figure something was off about us."

"Ah, c'mon, they're *humans*! How smart can they be?" Prince PD chuckled. "I think we could get away with it. And anytime we mess something up or act a little 'off,' well, we can blame it on too many bully sticks or too much playtime or too much kibble giving us a sore tummy or something. We can do this!"

"Well, maaaaaybe," Googly replied, looking down at his unwashed fur and too-long toenails. "But first of all, I need to get clean and you need to get dirty! And also . . . I've only ever had bully sticks when Great Auntie Sheila buys me one for Christmas after saving up all year, and I've never had enough kibble to get a tummy-ache, although it sounds like something I'd like! And you'd better be ready to do as much working as playing, because we don't have any servants so I help sweet Great Auntie Sheila with the chores every day."

"Chores! Work! Labor! Sounds great," Prince PD enthused. "I love trying new things! I'd love to give chores a go!"

After Prince PD scrubbed some soap into Googly's dirty fur and rinsed him off with the garden hose and clipped his long toenails with the nail clippers he found in one of Queen Mommy's girly things drawers, he declared his friend officially "clean and ready to rule!" Then he raced to the back gardens. Choosing a damp flower bed out of view of the palace windows, PD rolled and rolled in the wet dirt, making himself as unpresentable as Googly was when he first arrived.

After they laughingly paw-bumped one another, the two pugs swapped collars and agreed to meet up at the palace gates at five in the afternoon in a month's time. But just before leaving the palace, Prince PD went to the Royal Cabinet in the Royal Study and removed the Great Seal of Mommydom—representative of the monarch's authority to sign official documents affecting all villages under the Queen's realm—to ensure he could prove his standing should it ever be needed. After he buried it under his favorite marking tree, he wagged his curly tail in an excited goodbye, and off he went to Borsum, leaving Googly to play prince.

Googly, now squeaky clean and wearing Prince PD's bejeweled collar, took a deep breath and willed his thundering heart to slow down. *You're a prince now,* he told his scared self. *Act like a prince!* And he knew he'd need to do some great acting in order to pull this off. Googly took a moment to let his pug brain revisit his many viewings of the television series *Downton Abbey* as well as the many movies about royalty he and Great Auntie Sheila watched on their tiny television—films like *The King's Speech, The Queen, Ever After,* and more.

Doing his best imitation of Isis, the Grantham family's Labrador retriever, the pretend prince exited "his" bedroom and practiced a proud prance down the long, lushly carpeted hallway. The walls to either side displayed a mix of valuable paintings and portraits of the patriarchs and matriarchs of Queen Mommy's royal bloodline.

Googly-as-Prince PD approached what he knew would be his favorite room in the royal residence, the Royal Kitchen with its Royal Refrigerator filled with Royal Food, and began mentally preparing to start ruling things, like, um, the fridge. Just as he was about to push the door open with his paw, he was startled by an authoritative-sounding voice.

"M'lord! M'lord! What are you doing?" a matron in a maid's uniform called from behind him.

Googly's stomach flipped. *Am I caught? Does she know? Will I be beheaded?*

"It's not yet suppertime, Prince PD," said the none-the-wiser palace maid. "But if you don't tell Queen Mommy, I am willing to give you one of the large peanut butter biscuits I baked for your dessert."

His stomach calm again after quite the rollercoaster ride, a very relieved Googly turned to face the—*my?*—servant, whose name tag read *Mabel.* Wagging his tail with a happy confidence he did not feel, he spun in circles to show his glee over getting not just a biscuit, not just a homemade biscuit, not just a biscuit before he was supposed to get a biscuit, but his very most favorite *flavor* of biscuit: a *peanut butter* biscuit!

"Prince PD! What are you doing?" the dazed domestic demanded. "M'liege! You know that Queen Mommy disapproves of such commoner dog antics like spinning, jumping and getting the zoomies! Do I need to bring back the Royal Trainer? Now then! Behave as Queen Mommy likes, or no peanut butter biscuit before supper!"

Channeling Fortune, the pug owned by Emperor Napoleon de Bonaparte and his empress Josephine, Googly squared his haunches, raised his chin, and faced the housemaid. *I can do this!* he willed himself. *I can act all majestic and magnificent and spectacular and splendiferous and lofty and lordly like a prince would! I can, I can, I can!*

"PD? Are you going to stand there all day with that glazed expression, or are you going to wait by your Royal Bowl for your biscuit?" Mabel said, shaking her head but at least now looking a little less displeased. "Go sit by your bowl and I'll bring your shortbread shortly."

My bowl? My bowl? Googly resisted the urge to start spinning again, this time to do a 360 in search of said feeding vessel. *Other than Prince PD's bedroom, I don't exactly have the lay of the land yet. Um, I think I'd better take a tour and figure this place out.*

As Googly roamed the Royal Residence, doing a quick study of the home that would be his for the next month, the real Prince PD, now wearing Googly's shabby collar and *Googly* dog tag, was outside the palace recovering from a Royal Headache. When he had barked at the guards to express his displeasure with their abusive treatment of his new friend, the guards, not recognizing him as their prince, had actually grabbed him as they would a rabid dog and hurled him against a tree just beyond the gates.

Oh, my head! My head! he moaned as he staggered along the street. His environs rapidly receded in regality, the landscaping quickly going from nurtured to neglected, from lush to lacking. *Wow, this is where Googly lives? Yikes . . . But, no! I will not fear! This will be fun! For a whole month, I get to be a commoner! This will make me a more well-rounded, well-educated Prince PD! I will be able to relate to one and all as I help Mommy rule Mommydom! This will be fabulous!*

But as the day turned to night and the temperatures began dropping, the counterfeit commoner was no closer to finding the village of Borsum than when he set off from the palace. Prince PD started to feel less certain of this "fun" idea and more certain that he wanted to be in his Royal Bedroom, lying in his warm and cozy Royal Bed.

Just as he was about to give in to the temptation to race back to the security of Mommy Royale and the snuggly cuddles of Queen Mommy and the yummy Royal Kibble and Royal Yummies served to him by Maid Mabel, Prince PD lifted his hanging head to see a painted sign on a post just five or so feet in front of him, its words making him the smiliest he'd been in a while:

Village of Borsum
The Happiest Haven In Mommydom

Prince PD peered around, making sure he was unobserved. Then he spun and spun and spun, then jumped and jumped and jumped, then zoomed and zoomed and zoomed. For the next ten minutes, Prince PD acted very non-princely, breaking every rule of etiquette his trainer had taught him years ago.

If only Queen Mommy could see me now, he giggled as he started off on another zoom—but then he stopped, frozen mid-whoosh, as a menacing-looking mongrel suddenly stuck out a big paw aiming to trip Prince PD as he twirled to whizz the opposite way he'd been whizzing.

"Whoa, black pug. What do you think you're doing, tearing around *my* territory?" the unfriendly fleabag demanded. "You must not be from these parts. All the local dogs know that I, Ralph the Dog, rule Borsum. And all new dogs pay me three kibbles for the privilege of playing in my village!"

"Er, hi, Ralph!" Prince PD said, hoping to convey courage he didn't feel as he faced the fearsome cur. "Yes! I am new to Borsum and so happy to be here! I'm sorry that I don't have any kibble on me, but I assure you that if you can just give me a month, I'll give you a whole bag of kibble."

Ralph the Dog stared at the newcomer uncomprehendingly. "*What?* A *month?* Just who do you think you are, black pug?"

"Oh, sorry, where are my manners? Please pardon me, dear sir. My name is Prince PD! I come from the palace Mommy Royale, where I live with the Queen Mommy, who adopted me when I was a puppy. I'm sure you've sworn your allegiance to the Queen and likely visited the palace on a doggy daycare day excursion, and—"

"Oh, your majesty! Oh, m'lord! Oh, hail, Lord PD! Long may you reign!" said Ralph. Then he burst out laughing.

Ralph the Dog guffawed, clutching his mangy belly and rolling around on the ground, before getting serious. Really serious. Mad serious. Mean serious.

"Listen, whatever your real name is, black pug," Ralph the Dog growled. "I don't think you who you know who you are messing with, but I rule the dogs of this village, and you *will* present me with three kibbles by tomorrow noon if you think you are going to hang around these parts. Got it?"

Then, sticking his snout just inches from Prince PD's widening eyes, Ralph the Dog looked him up and down. "You know, you look a *lot* like that goofy Googly, this little black pug whose human is forever doting on him and making him feel he's not poor like other dogs in the village, telling him stupid stuff like 'Love is more important than extra toys and extra treats' and blah blah blah. That woman is forever spouting ridiculous nonsense like that."

Feigning ignorance of being acquainted with Googly, whose nametag thankfully had turned around during all his twirling and swirling, Prince PD said, "Wow, I'd love to see this alleged twin dog. Where, pray tell, does he live?"

"What am I, MapQuest?" Ralph the Dog snapped. "He lives with his Great Auntie Sheila in that little shack at the end of Bumbak Boulevard. But don't think you'll get kibble from them; they barely have enough for themselves.

"Now get out of here and be back at noon tomorrow with my kibble!"

And off Prince PD went in search of Googly's house.

Back at Mommy Royale, Googly, wearing the prince's bejeweled collar and managing to pass for Prince PD, was also managing to fake his way through the palace's customs and traditions and manners, thanks to both his watching of Downton Abbey and the short lesson he'd received during his time with his new friend. But apparently he wasn't pulling it off quite as well as he thought.

"PD, my sweet boy, what is with you lately?" a concerned Queen Mommy queried. "You're not yourself. You've twice forgotten where the kibble cabinet is; you've thrice snuck dog cookies from Maid Mabel's serving tray; you've wee-wee'd on the Royal Hall rug; and, the *coup de grâce*, you've also—ahem—passed gas three times in my presence, which is completely unacceptable and extremely *un*princely! Are you suffering from an illness? Shall I call in the Royal Veterinarian?"

Given that the last thing any dog wants is a visit from the vet, Googly redoubled his efforts to act as he assumed Prince PD would. He read up on Mommydom history and Mommy Royale rules and regulations; he memorized all the staff members' name tags; he tried harder to eat more slowly at meal and snack times; and he zoomed and spun only when he was certain no one was around. As his second day at the palace ended, Googly had convinced Queen Mommy and the palace staff that his mind was sound.

In just two days, the pauper pug had become a prince. Googly was enjoying the start of his month-long vacation as faux Prince PD. But he admitted to himself that he already missed home and the love of his Great Auntie Sheila.

Meanwhile, back in Borsum, Great Auntie Sheila was beside herself with worry. Her prized pug had gone missing two whole days now, and she was fearing the worst. She knew there were some true junkyard dogs living nearby, like that ferocious, fearsome Ralph the Dog who was forever fighting any canine that crossed his path. Not to mention the many dognapers in this low-income area who would be only too thrilled to snatch Googly off the streets and sell her darling dog to the highest bidder.

"Oh dear, oh dear, oh dear," the poor paralyzed-with-fear woman pondered as she paced. "What if he is lying somewhere bruised and bleeding after being beaten by big bad Ralph the Dog? What if some dognaper has him in a van that's headed to some puppy mill?

"Oh, what to do? What to do? *What to do?!*"

Just as Great Auntie Sheila hung her head to sob, there came a soft tap at the front door. She hurried to the door, fearing it was the pound officer or someone else with bad news about her Googly. But no . . . it was Googly himself! And he looked . . . not only well but oddly clean and groomed, with the glossiest coat she'd ever seen on a dog.

"My goodness, Googly!" Great Auntie Sheila exclaimed, lifting what she thought was her little pug into her arms and hugging him tightly. "Where have you been? I've been worried sick!" Then she added, giggling, "And did some nice neighbor treat you to a spa day? Or did you take a dip in the lake? I've never seen you so squeaky clean and shiny! But no matter, you're home now. Let's get you inside! I'll bet you're starving!"

Doing his best to mimic the Googly characteristics he'd studied when the two dogs were together in his Royal Bedroom, Prince PD hoped he was pulling off posing as his pug pal, just as he hoped Googly was acting convincingly princely back at Mommy Royale. Moments later, he was offered a fun opportunity to see if his acting was up to snuff.

"Oh, how I've missed you, Googly; I just don't laugh as much when you're not here to entertain me," Great Auntie Sheila said smilingly. "Show me your tricks! Chase your tail, Googly! Let's see how many twirls you can do before you fall over from dizziness! Last week you were up to two full minutes before you threw up your kibble.

"Okay, ready . . . GO!"

Wait, what? I am allowed to spin? Prince PD mused incredulously. *Queen Mommy's trainers taught me never to spin! never to zoom! never to jump! Is this woman saying I can whirligig and corkscrew and pirouette and pinwheel around like a, like a, a, a* commoner *dog?*

Leaping into the air, Prince PD thought with glee, *I've always wanted to play with the commoner dogs! I've always envied the commoner dogs! They get to just "be" and not have to be all princey perfect all the time! This is the best playtime ever!*

As Prince-PD-as-Googly pretended to be a circus clown, entertaining "his" Great Auntie Sheila with spins and leaps and zooms and even attempting to juggle three of the homemade dog cookies the kind woman had baked as she prayed for her missing pug to come home, Googly-as-Prince-PD was nursing his first-ever bellyache. Back at Mommy Royale, the furry faux royal was partaking in types of feasts he hadn't known existed.

I thought the Thanksgiving dinner stories my dog pals and I read about back home were just fables, just folklore, thought Googly. *It feels like every meal here is Thanksgiving! The last time I felt this full was that time the Chewy truck overturned near our house and three bags of kibble burst open all over the street. And this is better!*

"Prince PD? Earth to Prince PD!" Googly snapped out of his daydream to find Queen Mommy inches away, staring into his face. "I've been saying your name for three minutes! I said, it's time for your king lessons. I won't be around forever, you know; one day this realm will be yours."

Queen Mommy rang the bell in her hand. "Maid Mabel!" she called. "Please summon the Royal Instructors. It's time for the prince's refinement and manners course, followed by his Royal Customs and History lesson. And would you please stop sneaking him cookies during class? I need him focused on the teacher; yesterday he was acting as if he had never had a session at all! He seemed to have forgotten everything he has been taught this whole year!"

And on things went for the remaining weeks that the two pugs lived in one another's homes. Prince-PD-as-Googly enjoyed being a commoner dog, playing and goofing around when not helping Great Auntie Sheila with the many daily chores, and enjoying having no lessons nor realm responsibilities, even if he didn't get the amount of cookies and bully sticks and toys he was used to. And Googly-as-Prince-PD enjoyed privilege and a swollen belly, even if it came with sitting in on court judgments, studying daily for a kingship he never would actually assume, and having to act more "proper" than a village dog would ever act.

Finally the time clock on the ruse ran out. As planned a month prior in Prince PD's Royal Bedroom, it was time for Prince PD to leave the loving warmth of Great Auntie Sheila and head home to the wealth of his secure but responsibility-laden future. And it was time for Googly to bid adieu to scrumptious succulence at suppertime and velvet dog beds and king training and return to being poor but content. Both dogs were sad to leave their temporary homes and newly beloved temporary caregivers but happy to go back to the lives they knew and also enjoyed, despite their perceived negatives.

Googly waited until the three o'clock hour of Queen Mommy's Royal Nap. After watching her chest rise and fall a dozen times to ensure she was in Royal Slumber, Googly grabbed a baggie filled with Maid Mabel's warm-from-the-oven peanut butter dog cookies, raced down the grand Royal Hall, and quietly pushed open the heavy fortified-with-iron oak door. Googly quickly padded all the way down the long drive to the outer gates, and just when he was pushing them open with his forepaws . . .

"M'lord! M'lord! Where are you off to? Surely you are not racing off to do some tomfoolery and ballyhoo when it's your Royal Naptime?"

Googly spun around, nearly flinging the baggie of cookies, and locked eyes with an out-of-breath Maid Mabel, who happened to be out in the Royal Garden hanging the Queen Mommy's Royal Bloomers to dry.

Knowing the jig needed to be up, Googly took a deep breath, removed Prince PD's bejeweled collar, and put his forepaws together in an "arrest me" pose.

"Oh, silly Prince PD, don't worry," Maid Mabel chuckled. "I won't tattle on you. Now put your collar back on and come along."

Googly desperately needed a diversion so that he could make another run for it. *Break one rule, break them all,* he thought, and he started spinning, zooming and jumping all around. Then he put his now dirty paws right on a very stunned Maid Mabel's bleached white apron. And as the attempt to flee continued . . .

. . . Down the way in the village of Borsum, Prince PD was attempting to make a getaway of his own. After getting a tight hug from Great Auntie Sheila and watching her put the bit of grocery money and food coupons into her pocket and set off to the shops, Prince PD took a final look around the happy little haven and opened the front door . . .

. . . only to see that hound from Hades, Ralph the Dog, hanging out on the corner with some other mean-looking, mangy mutts. But the prince needed to get back to the palace by the agreed-upon afternoon hour, and so, taking a deep breath, he started running and running and running . . . until *smack!* He landed flat on his face on the other side of Ralph the Dog's just-extended forepaw.

"Oh, lookie here, boys," the hoodlum hound howled in mocking laughter. "It's the so-called 'Prince,' who of course is none other than goofball Googly. Where ya off to, goof face?"

Prince PD righted himself and attempted to put up a brave front to the curs circled around him. "I am, um, just out for a walk. Um, I mean, I am going to the market to get your three kibbles, Ralph. I am so sorry it's late. I had to do chores to earn the money."

"You'd better not be lying to me, Googly," Ralph the Dog sneered. "In fact, I think I'll just follow you to make certain you . . ."

But Prince-PD-as-Googly wasn't listening; he *had* to get home by five! He suddenly bolted off toward Mommy Royale, with Ralph the Dog so close behind he was nearly nipping at his tail. The chase went on for miles, with Prince PD hoping, hoping, hoping to make it home as he hot-footed it.

And then there it was: Mommy Royale, his palatial home! Such a happy sight. Except . . . *Wait,* puzzled Prince PD— *what is Googly still doing here? Why is he at the gates surrounded by Maid Mabel and the Royal Guards? He should be nearly back to Borsum by now!*

Although Prince PD had gained some ground on Ralph the Dog, his several moments staring at the activity at the palace gates let the bully catch up. Prince PD bunched his shoulders into himself, waiting for the blow that was surely coming. . . .

But it didn't. He turned to see Ralph the Dog frozen to his spot behind him, rotating his head from the prince to the real Googly just several yards away.

"What on *Earth* is going on?" the confused cur questioned. "One Googly is bad enough! How do you have a twin I didn't know about? And *what* is he *doing* at Mommy Royale?"

Meanwhile, at the gates, Googly had removed his friend's bejeweled collar and was trying to explain to Maid Mabel and the guards—none of whom spoke dog—that he was not actually the prince. All they could understand was that "the prince" seemed to be losing his Royal Mind; he was spinning in circles and jumping up and down in an attempt to prevent the collar's reattachment as well as to avoid being grabbed and taken back inside.

"Googly! Answer me!" demanded Ralph the Dog. "Who is that? What is he doing here?"

But Prince PD didn't have time to catch his nemesis up on the happenings of the past month. He had to help his friend! And get home again to his Mommy! So he raced as fast as his little pug legs would carry him down the way to the gates and skidded to a halt right at the shuffling legs of Maid Mabel, who was so focused on grabbing the lightning-quick Googly that she didn't realize Prince PD was there until Googly stopped dancing about and yipped with glee.

It was hard to say who looked more confused: Maid Mabel and the guards, or Ralph the Dog. The guards, however, obedient to their oath to protect Queen Mommy, seized Prince PD, thinking he was a threat to what they *assumed* was Prince PD. Googly, scared for the fate of his friend and at a loss for how to prevent a predictably poor outcome, for the first time in his life was happy to see his nemesis Ralph the Dog. The latter, knowing only that there were too many Googlys for his liking and deciding he should be the one doling out punishment, grabbed the kilt of the Royal Guard holding Prince PD, and yanked it right off, causing the guard to drop the prince . . .

. . . who, to the surprise of everyone but Googly, raced away from the group—but not to escape. Instead, he sprinted to that favorite tree he had visited when this all began and dug up the Great Seal. As he ran back with it in his teeth, he was relieved to see a huge smile widening on Maid Mabel's face.

"M'lord! M'lord!" she cried as Prince PD leaped into her arms and she took the seal. "Is it really you?" And her question was answered moments later when Googly knelt before his friend with the royal dog tag in his teeth and as Prince

PD jumped down and the two exchanged neckwear. The friends nuzzled noses and cried happy howls, making clear to all around them that they were canine compadres who had pulled a fast one on everyone from Queen Mommy on down.

And speaking of Queen Mommy . . .

"What is all this racket? What is all this commotion? What is all this . . ." Queen Mommy stood just inside of gates, scratching her Royal Head in disbelief. "Why am I seeing two Prince PDs?"

Maid Mabel stepped forward and curtsied. "M'queen. Allow me. The darling little pug who has lived with us the past month certainly *is* darling, but he is not *your* darling. Seems the Prince and his new friend have shown us the truth in the saying *Boys will be boys.* They certainly have had their fun putting one over on us."

Everyone held their collective breath as Queen Mommy stared at the real and faux princes, who were standing abreast awaiting a Royal Chewing Out. And not the kind of chewing that included their beloved bully sticks, either.

But punishment was the furthest thing from Queen Mommy's Royal Mind.

"Prince PD, I have loved you and spoiled you, but I now see I haven't let you be a little boy dog like other little boy dogs. When your doppelgänger here arrived a month ago, I was nonplussed by what certainly were crude manners—well, at least by Royal Standards. I see now that spinning and jumping and, Lord save me, barking aren't always bad. Sometimes, maybe most times, they mean *fun* times.

"I love you, little PD. And you've shown me every day that you love me," Queen Mommy added smilingly. "But it took this switcheroo of yours for me to see that there should be at least as much Royal Playtime as Royal Duty Time."

Upon hearing those heartfelt words, a wet-eyed Prince PD leaped up in the most un-royal way and licked and licked and licked Queen Mommy's right cheek. And the next second, he was joined by his partner in pranks, Googly, who leaped and licked and licked and licked the Queen's left cheek. Queen Mommy let out an un-royal roar of raucous laughter, drawing slack-jawed stares from Maid Mabel and all the guards, who at first tentatively and then fully committedly joined in the laughter.

The sole silent one in the crowd was the still-stupefied stinker, Ralph the Dog.

"Would someone *please* tell me what's going *on*?" he blared, baring teeth that for once were scaring no one, only drawing the eyes of guards who acted quickly to fulfill their "protect Queen Mommy" mandate. The next thing ruffian Ralph the Dog knew, he was handcuffed to the gate, cowering cringingly and looking nothing like the bulldozing bully he was known for being.

A week later, Googly was back in his happy home in the loving arms of his Great Auntie Sheila. As the dear woman presented her precious pug with the surprise bully stick she'd purchased using pinched pennies, there came a knock at the door. To the shock of them both, it was none other than Prince PD and Maid Mabel.

"G'day, Miss," Maid Mabel said as she curtsied to a surprised Great Auntie Sheila, who'd certainly never been curtsied to in her life. "I'm here with news—news that I hope will make you and Prince PD's favorite friend Googly here very happy indeed.

"Seems Prince PD is very lonely for a real friend, a friend like Googly. So the Queen Mommy requests the honor of your lifelong presence in your own wing at Mommy Royale. If you accept, you forever will have plenty to eat and warm, comfortable beds, and Googly will be the prince's ward and will be under the protection of the prince and the palace.

"Um, not that he'll need it," Maid Mabel added, laughing. "Ralph the Dog won't be causing trouble. He currently is serving two months in the palace dungeon, dining on generic-brand kibble and no bully sticks at all, as punishment for his years of harassment of Ward Googly." Then she winked. "And don't pity him. The benevolent Queen Mommy is making sure even Ralph the Dog is treated humanely during his detention, much to the disappointment of Prince PD."

Great Auntie Sheila and Googly looked around at their happy, albeit tiny home, each no doubt thinking of their joyful moments there together. Just as Googly assumed she'd turn down the offer, Great Auntie Sheila beamed the biggest grin he'd seen to date.

"Well . . . gee, I guess," Great Auntie Sheila deadpanned before breaking into laughter. "I do love Borsum, and we've managed just fine, surviving as much on love as on creature comforts. But whaddaya say, Googly? You wanna see how 'the other half' lives for a while? From what I've heard so far about this Queen Mommy, I am convinced you can be poor and kind as well as rich and kind. Or you can be poor and unkind as well as rich and unkind.

"Queen Mommy has shown me that just because you are in a palace doesn't always mean you are blind and deaf to the suffering of those less fortunate.

"Now let's get packing and start enjoying daily bully sticks for you and a bit of the life of leisure for your Great Auntie. And Googly, don't forget to get Royal Permission to spin, jump and leap, for goodness' sake!"

(PD note: This PD Fairy Tail is based on The Prince and the Pauper *by Mark Twain. The literary analyst people say the story's lessons are that appearances are deceiving and that one's true nobility and true wealth come from within, and that our value in this world should be based not on social status but rather on our character and actions. Nope. Wrong again. The moral is that Ralph the Dog needs to be locked in a dungeon. And If I can sneak around the publisher and edit this later, Ralph the Dog sure will be serving more than two stupid months!)*

Chapter Six

PD AND THE BEANSTALK

𝕴𝖓 𝕬 𝕷𝖆𝖓𝖉 𝕱𝖆𝖗, 𝕱𝖆𝖗 𝕬𝖜𝖆𝖞 there lived a poor country pug named PD. The impoverished pug owned nothing but a sickly, aging cow named Bessie, who thankfully was still able to produce enough milk to nourish the down-and-out dog. Farmer Charlie let them live in a rented stall on his tiny farm and gave PD an occasional chicken dinner as long as PD did chores for him.

One day a leprechaun approached PD and his skinny cow companion at the farm. The wizened and weathered gnome offered PD a handful of what he swore were "magical" beans in exchange for the cow. While PD was sad to bid adieu to his beloved bovine, he couldn't resist owning something that was magical, and so he quickly made the swap.

For days, PD just stared at the beans. He alternated between excitement over owning something "magical," sadness over missing his bovine buddy, and fear that he could run out of milk before the beans worked their wizardry and fostered untold fortune.

But the beans did nothing, and after a week of waiting, PD felt that Fat City was as far off as his old farm friend.

How can these little bitty beans lead to a better life for a penniless pug? What was I thinking? the doggy deliberated. *Now I don't have Bessie the cow to provide milk, and I'm too poor to get another cow. Soon I'll waste away.*

PD began agitatedly spinning in circles—not the happy sort of circles he did occasionally to make Farmer Charlie grin, but the sort that a dog (and maybe a human, for that matter) might do when fretting about the future. And the more he revolved, the more he regretted listening to the puck who he now felt had punked him.

I had a cow! Now I have nothing but a stupid handful of stupid beans! he thought bitterly. *Gee, maybe these—HA!—"magical" beans will "magically" produce a "magical" lifetime supply of suppers for me and Farmer Charlie.*

Now angry with himself, PD grabbed the beans in his tiny paw and threw them as far as that little forefoot could throw. Then he went home to his farm stall and, staring at the photo of Bessie and him that Farmer Charlie had taken and tacked on the stall wall, PD tossed and turned on his bed of hay and cried himself to sleep.

Meanwhile, in a patch of dirt at the edge of the farm, the allegedly magical beans were actually manifesting a bit of magic! Unbeknownst to the self-pitying pug, the tossed beans supernaturally buried themselves, seeking the moisture just beneath the surface . . .

Two weeks later, PD was hard at work feeding Farmer Charlie's chickens, fertilizing and harvesting the crops, tuning up the tractor, and fixing the fence. All the while, he continued beating himself up, wondering why he had allowed himself to be fooled by that fraudster faerie into actually believing a handful of beans could have magical properties.

I feel so hopeless, he thought. *What's the point of this life of cowlessness and drudgery? I wish God would just take me to Heaven right now. I wish that song "Stairway to Heaven" would play, and a stairway would . . .*

Suddenly PD stopped ruminating. He heard a low, deep rumble and a bit of crackling and creaking, just loud enough to be picked up by his button pug ears. *Where are those sounds coming from?* he wondered, looking around the farm. *It's not thunder; it's not a passing tractor. Sadly, it's not my cow coming home. What's going on?*

He didn't have to wonder long. As he rotated his large pug head, his googly eyes goggled as he gawked until they were googling so wide that he looked like a squashed frog. Because about twenty feet down the way, where he'd hurled the beans . . . well, something . . . something—*er, magical?*—was happening! Somehow, that handful of beans had grown into a ginormous, gigantic beanstalk!

Suddenly PD was no longer anxious to go home to Heaven before his pugly time on Earth was up. He was no longer eager to go gently into that good night or whatever those goofball human poets poeted about. *No!* Now he wanted to cash in on whatever was happening with his beans—his! His! *His* beans! Staring up at the massive beanstalk, he momentarily forgot his broken heart over his cashed-in cow.

Tentatively, cautiously, uncertainly, PD approached the towering, imposing plant, noting how its enormity caused everything around it to look Lilliputian in comparison. Even the aging oak tree he'd just marked with his wee-wee looked somehow small next to the massive stalk. But what was more amazing was that the huge plant appeared to reach all the way to the sky! Into the clouds! To the very heavens!

How is this even possible? PD wondered, staring through eyes as gargantuan as those of a tarsier. Or a giant squid. Or at least a tree frog. *It's a bean behemoth! Is it even sensible to think that my pawful of beans became this stratospheric stem?*

Snapping out of his gaping and gawking, PD put his forelimbs around the base of the plant and—allowing his curiosity to overtake his fear—began to climb. Up and up he ascended, his furry little body tightly hugging the stalk. One forepaw pulled, one hind paw pushed, up and up he went, and then . . .

Wow! PD's round pug head emerged above the clouds, and he was shocked to discover a whole little town in the sky, at the center of which stood a resplendent, radiant white castle. *Whoa!* thought PD. *Magical beans, indeed!*

But then it occurred to him that despite the magicalness of this moment, he was no closer to having food or fortune than before he'd traded away his dear cow. *C'mon, PD! Eyes on the prize,* he thought. *Let's see if those leprechauns really do give gold at the end of the rainbow. Er, end of the stalk, I guess.*

PD started exploring this mystical mini metropolis in the clouds, his hopes high that he would find food. Suddenly sensing he was not alone, he spun around to find that dog-gone leprechaun from Earth looking down at him from a tree and grinning widely.

"Ah, little PD! I thought I might find you here," the imp said. "Most folks accept my beans but lose faith in the magic part. So they toss the beans away, just like you did.

"But at least you, PD, believed enough in magic to climb the stalk all the way to the sky. So let's see if you have enough belief in magic—and in *yourself*—to find sustenance to fill your belly to its brim!"

And with that, the little man disappeared, leaving a hungry and perplexed PD standing outside the imposing castle. Mustering his courage, PD pushed open the door and went inside. An enchanting aroma led him to the castle kitchen, where he was giddy to see a big bowl of kibble and three big, sloppy soup bones on a plate. PD's snaggletooth smile gleamed as he thought of filling his rumbling belly.

But within seconds, that smile became a grimace. Because he was greeted—and not in a "Hiya-happy-to-know-you" way—by the most menacing-looking Rottweiler he'd ever laid his googly eyes on. The deep-set almond eyes staring back at him were accompanied by forty-two terrifying, slobbery teeth, leading PD to one conclusion:

I need to get out of here!

PD turned tail and was about to flee when he heard something that froze him in place in his paw prints.

"Fee Fi Fo Fug! I smell the stink of an unwashed pug! Be he fat or be he thin, I . . ."

PD didn't want to wait for the end of the couplet, which he was certain was just the start of an epic poem of suffering and tragedy . . . *his* suffering and tragedy! He had to *go! Now!!*

But . . . of course, being an impoverished, ravenously hungry dog, PD couldn't resist grabbing one of the savory-looking soup bones off the Rottweiler's plate before hightailing it out of the castle, down the beanstalk, and back to the farm.

Farmer Charlie looked up from his corn shucking and saw his dog friend racing home. Having no idea what PD had just gone through, the farmer was happy to see the big bone. He smiled, knowing it meant the little canine would have enough calories for a while.

"Where ya been, little buddy?" Farmer Charlie asked, patting the still very traumatized pug. "My, oh my! You're shaking and panting so hard, PD! You okay?"

No I am not okay! PD thought as he willed his thundering heart to slow. *I just narrowly escaped being eaten by a Rottweiler! At least I got a couple of days' dinner out of my risky romp to that castle in the air.*

That night, as he carefully chomped on the soup bone—being a farm dog, he had learned from Farmer Charlie not to let a bone splinter into shards that could get wedged between his teeth or jaws—PD thought about his future. He still had no cow and so no milk source. The bone he was gnawing was delicious, but once it was gone, there would be no more.

Wait. Unless . . .

There are at least two more soup bones in that kitchen, PD mused, salivating over both the bone he was chewing on and the mere thought of more. *Thanks to that little elf, I have my own ladder to a castle in the sky! It would be silly of me not to go back! I could get more bones—and who knows what else is in that kitchen! That Rottweiler looked plenty well fed!*

I just have to avoid getting eaten . . .

The next day, PD mustered more courage than that time he barked at those wolves that were sniffing around Farmer Charlie's chicken coop, and he again ascended the bean stalk. *Those wolves were nothing,* he thought, his forelegs shaking as he climbed. *This Rottweiler would gobble them and me right up without his heart rate raising a single beat. But I can't not go to the castle! I need food! And I own this stalk, doggone it!*

PD crept from the cloud opening to the nearby castle. As silent as that mouse that kept mousing around Farmer Charlie's cheese shelf, PD slowly pushed open the massive oak doors and stealthily entered, craning his round pug head as far forward as he could to make sure the scary Rottweiler wasn't there to greet him this time.

Entering the kitchen—and seeing the coast was clear—the little farm dog peered around, seeking out any yummy-looking sustenance he could carry in the small knapsack he had secured to his strong back. Approaching the huge refrigerator, PD made sure once more that he was alone. Then, tempting fate, he opened its stainless-steel door and . . .

WHOA! Look at all this food, thought PD. *It's like a dog's fantasy fridge! There's Greek yogurt, beef sticks, hot dogs! Boiled chicken, cheese, and so much more! This is more food than Farmer Charlie and I have ever seen in one setting!*

His googly eyes bigger even than his growling tummy, PD was just opening his knapsack to load it up with all the goodies it could hold when he heard the last thing he wanted to hear while he was so quietly going about his, um, food borrowing: toenails tapping on the kitchen floor. They belonged to the fearsome-looking Rottweiler, who had just entered his kitchen to find the same black pug he'd found there the day prior.

And while PD already was terrified just seeing the dreaded dog, his fear increased tenfold when the clicking claws were followed, again, by the start of that frightening poem:

"Fee Fi Fo Fug! I smell the stink of an unwashed pug! Be he fat or be he thin, I . . ."

Petrified PD reached deep within his little pug body for fortitude he didn't feel. He decided, *I didn't risk my little life to go home with nothing. I need to bring some of that yummy food home! I need food!*

Channeling David facing Goliath, PD prayed the approaching dog wouldn't reach him before he got what he'd come for. He reached into the open refrigerator door and, without worrying what he was grabbing, quickly swiped some foodstuffs toward and over the edge of a shelf and hoped a dozen or so delectable dog delights would make it into his bag.

Then, seconds before the running Rottweiler reached him, PD lickedysplitted it out of the castle and onto the beanstalk and scooted down quicker than any pug ever scooted.

Farmer Charlie again happened to be outside, this time tilling the soil for the coming season's plantings, when PD came tearing down the lane leading to the farm.

"Good grief, little friend! Where's the fire?" the farmer guffawed, again having no idea what his companion had just gone through in the castle in the sky. "You sure are struggling with that bag. Let me help you." Farmer Charlie's eyes widened at the weight of PD's knapsack as he hefted it onto his shoulder and carried it inside his primitive country home.

"Wow! What do we have here?" said the farmer with a stupefied stare. "Did you stick up Grocer Gary? I mean, yogurt, beef sticks, cheese! This is a lot of food, PD! I am going to assume you came about this honestly and we can enjoy these delicious-looking goodies guilt-free."

Looking anywhere but into the farmer's face, PD wagged his tail—*okay, maybe the teensiest bit fibbingly,* he admitted to himself—and proceeded to take the food that had minutes earlier been in the Rottweiler's refrigerator and placed it in Farmer Charlie's icebox. There was enough food that it took him a happily spent half hour to arrange everything on the hitherto nearly barren shelves.

That was a close call, PD thought an hour later as he and Farmer Charlie dug into the largest meal consisting of the most wonderful fare they'd eaten since that Thanksgiving at Grocer Gary's home. *I need to be content with the food I got today,* PD thought as they noshed. *It's no cow; it won't provide continuous comestibles, but it's good for a while, and I need to be grateful for it.*

But the next morning when PD woke and his belly had finally finished digesting the big meal, PD started daydreaming about going back to the castle. He drooled as he imagined the remaining food in the Rottweiler's refrigerator and decided that it would be foolish not to make one more foray into the firmament and grab more grub.

Once again strapping his knapsack to his broad back, PD made sure Farmer Charlie was otherwise occupied, then hurriedly padded back to the beanstalk and . . . up he went!

This time, though—to the furry little refrigerator raider's surprise—he found the fearsome face of what he believed to be his most frightening foe waiting for him right next to the cloud opening. As PD stared into the Rottweiler's imposing face, his heart pounded so hard he thought surely it would be heard clear back at the farm.

PD cowered. And then he tried to recall the prayers Farmer Charlie recited in the evenings: petitions for blessings and help from God. *I'm so near Heaven,* PD thought, *maybe God will be able to hear me better! Please, God, HELP ME!*

Alas, God apparently was taking a celestial snooze—because no help came, only that dreaded poem!

"Fee Fi Fo Fug! I smell the stink of an unwashed pug! Be he fat or be he thin . . ."

PD squeezed his eyes shut, figuring he soon would know how that Old Testament guy Jonah felt in the belly of that whale. *I stole that dog's dinner, and now I get to be his dinner,* thought PD sadly. *This is it. This is the end. I won't see Farmer Charlie or the hens or my other farm friends ever again. It's time to be eaten, because . . .*

". . . I will make a friend of him."

PD couldn't believe his button ears. This frightening, fearsome, fierce, feral-looking dog didn't want to eat him; he wanted to *play* with him!

"I'm Rory Rottweiler. Welcome to my castle," the huge dog said before looking down and making what sounded like a sad sniffle. "I live alone here in the sky. My only regular occasional visitor is Larry Leprechaun. Years ago, I asked him to bring me a friend with whom I could play and share my food and toys.

"But every dog who has come takes one look at me and decides I mean him harm. And every time, they run away without giving me a chance to say hello and extend my paw in friendship.

"Yesterday you were the first-ever dog to brave coming back. So I pressed my paws together and prayed you'd come one more time. And I have been waiting there by the cloud entrance ever since."

PD gaped, struggling to believe he wasn't going to be the main course of the huge dog's pug picnic. "Wait," he said. "You mean you don't want to eat me?"

The Rottweiler roared a raucous laugh. "Eat you? Good heavens, no!" Leaning forward to read the pug's dog tag, he continued, "PD, I don't want you to be my *feast*. I want you to be my *friend*. Every dog is scared of me. So I don't have any friends. Will you please be my friend, little PD?"

PD was the happiest he'd remembered being since Grocer Gary brought them the overage he'd gotten from the butcher. He wasn't going home to Heaven—yet! He was going home to the farm, and now he was going to bring a new friend with him!

"I would love to be your friend, Rory! I am so sorry I assumed by your looks that you were a mean monster dog. Just because you look formidable doesn't mean you are formidable. You are gentle and just as friendly as me!

"I'm sorry I didn't give you a chance. Please forgive me."

"Forgiven!" Rory said, laughing. "Now, enough groveling! Let's get to the grub!" And off they ran to the big refrigerator for the first of many feasts.

And over the months and years, PD Pug and Rory Rottweiler became the closest of canine compadres. Rory shared from his overflowing food stores, while PD and Farmer Charlie welcomed him into their little farm family and "shared" the chores that strong Rory was only too happy to help with.

And maybe the happiest one of all was Larry Leprechaun, who shocked the group one fine Spring day by coming to the farm holding a long rope, the end of which was looped around the neck of PD's old cow, Bessie! And she didn't look old and sickly anymore, either!

"PD," said Larry, "you are the only dog who passed the test. You did something meaningful with the magical beans you traded your cow for. You made Rory the smiliest Rottweiler ever. You gave away your security for something much better: joy in the heart of another.

"So let me give you some joy. Bessie here ate some magical beans of her own. This batch of beans turned back time, and now she is young again and able to produce more healthy milk than ever before. And she is yours again to cherish."

The whole group cheered and danced around. And as the little man disappeared up the beanstalk, up, up and away, PD realized that true wealth has nothing to do with possessions but rather comes from the things we can't buy: friends and family and simple pleasures.

But, c'mon, a lifetime of chowing down Rory's chow wasn't bad, either.

(*PD note: This PD Fairy Tail is based on the old English tale "Jack and the Beanstalk," whose first version is credited to J. Roberts. In the original, Jack faces a mean giant, whereas I faced what turned out to be a very* nice *giant. You likely think the moral of my tale is to not judge a book—or a Rottweiler—by its cover. Or maybe don't break and enter. Or maybe don't break and enter and also steal. Or maybe don't be a glutton. Or maybe don't sell the supplier of your meals for some beans. No! The moral is that if you're so hungry you could faint and you find a refrigerator stocked with yummy nummy numnums, fill your knapsack and get out of Dodge pronto. And then maybe go back for seconds. Obviously.*)

Chapter Seven

PD HOOD AND HIS MERRY MUTTS

𝕴𝖓 𝕿𝖍𝖊 𝕯𝖆𝖞𝖘 𝕺𝖋 𝖄𝖔𝖗𝖊 in the District of Dogville, in a time when the "haves" had more consumables than they could ever consume and the "have-nots" had nary a nugget of nourishment, there lived a pug named PD Hood.

Dogville was the largest part of the Greater Homeland of Hound, which was ruled by Sheriff Ralph the Dog. Sheriff Ralph was a cruel ruler, a tyrant who burdened the middle and lower classes of Hound with crushing kibble customs and intolerable toy taxation. And as mean as he was to those without means, he was more than magnanimous in his favoritism to the citizens of Dogville's rich neighborhood, Dogville Estates. The wealthy dogs of Dogville Estates happily kept the corrupt cur Sheriff Ralph in office in exchange for the free trees and bushes his city hall gardeners planted outside their mansions and the frosted cookies he surreptitiously slipped through their doggie door flaps.

Unfortunately for PD Hood, his own taxes were even higher than those of his pals in middle-class Dogville Digs, going back to a rivalry with the sheriff that began in their boyhood.

PD Hood in his puppy days was quite the sportsdog, known for his excellence in marksmanship—peeing marksmanship, that is—as well as for his deftness in bully-stick dueling matches. He was unmatched in both the bullseye aim of his weewee and the accuracy of his bully sword. And, as unmatched as PD Hood was in athleticism, he had an equally rosy reputation for his giving heart, often sharing his kibble and toys with his friends.

Ralph the Dog, on the other paw, even in his tot times had a rascally reputation. He and a few other despicable dirtbags picked fights with the other young dogs of Dogville; young Ralph the Dog soon became known as Dogville's scampiest scoundrel.

On PD Hood's third birthday, his pal Charlie Chihuahua challenged the whiz wizzer to hit a tree from a distance of ten feet. PD Hood assumed a stance at the specified distance from the targeted tree, raised his left hind leg, and hit the target . . . only to find that this tree belonged to Ralph the Dog's father, Ralph Senior, who was then Sheriff of Dogville. Finding the pug's bullseye marking on the bole of their beloved beechwood, both Sheriff Ralph the Dog and his son vowed eternal enmity with PD Hood. The elder Sheriff Ralph sentenced PD Hood to one month in the frightening and forbidding Furry Forest, and he tripled his taxation.

After surviving the month in Furry Forest thanks to his skills in digging for bugs and burying himself under warm leaves at bedtime, PD Hood returned to his home in middle-class Dogville Digs. PD Hood and his canine chums enjoyed a good life, hanging in their neighborhoods or at the local dog park or the nearby doggie daycare center. They called themselves the Merry Mutts, and, while not enjoying the spoils of the dwellers of wealthy Dogville Estates, they nevertheless never worried about having enough kibble to eat or enough toys to play with.

The Merry Mutts also enjoyed the wisdom shared and good examples set by their elders, the long-in-the-canine canines of Dogville Digs. The older dogs taught PD Hood and the other young dogs many good dog lessons, one of which was the importance of charity and kindness to those in need. The most revered of the elders, Friar Foxhound, shared stories of starving strays who were said to live at a landfill on the other side of Hound.

PD Hood had never seen a dog-food-deprived dog, and he often found himself reflecting on the rumored reality of pooch poverty. He sometimes spoke about it with his sidekick, Little John Jämthund (ironically named, as the Jämthund breed outweighs pugs by a good fifty pounds).

"How can there be dogs who are hungry and have no toys, Little John?" PD Hood would ask incredulously.

"I agree!" Little John Jämthund would respond. "I mean, we aren't rich like the hoity-toity hounds in Dogville Estates, but I have kibble and four toys! Friar Foxhound can't be right! I have never seen an actual hungry dog."

These stories weighed on the mind and heart of good-hearted PD Hood. *How can there be dogs that are homeless and foodless and toyless?* he would think. *That would be terrible! I bet Friar Foxhound and the other old dogs are just joshing around. Like when they told all us youngsters to bring our cookies to them so they could 'test them for toxins.' Ha! We caught on to that one!*

But the question of whether there were in fact poor dogs living at the landfill niggled at PD Hood's mind, causing him to wonder why the elders would invent something so awful.

One day while out on a walkie, PD Hood's curiosity got the better of him, and he decided to venture out to the deserted, dumpy, derelict district of Dogville where the landfill was located to see for himself these alleged uncared-for canines.

As he walked for blocks and blocks, as the landscape changed from green and well-maintained to brown and trash-filled and neglected, PD Hood was so lost in thought that he didn't realize he was approaching the Dogville landfill. He looked up just in time to stop his round head from bonking into a dilapidated sign that was hanging on one hinge, swinging a bit in the afternoon breeze.

The tilted metal sign read:

DOGVILLE DUMP
No Admittance Other Than Licensed Dogville Garbage Collectors!
By Order Of Sheriff Ralph The Dog!

Nervously looking around and ascertaining that he was alone, PD Hood took a deep breath of the foul-smelling air and pushed on the hinged gate. It swung forward with little resistance, and moments later the little pug entered the dumping ground and tremulously trod toward the reeking crater that was filled to overflowing with the Greater Homeland of Hound's household refuse and non-hazardous sludge and waste.

Peeyew! thought PD Hood as he ventured toward the reeking rubbish. *Good thing I won't be here long; imagine* living *in this stink! Good thing no dogs actually* do*! How silly I was to even wonder, because obviously . . .*

"Grrrrrr! Grrrrrrrrrrrrrr!! Grrrrrrrrrrrrrrrrrrrrr!!!"

PD Hood froze mid-thought as the most bloodcurdling noise he'd ever heard gripped his very soul. He was too terrified to move, let alone look for the source of the soul-chilling sound. He stared at his forepaws, willing himself to pug up and face the fear.

"Who do you think you are, pug intruder?" came a loud, forbidding voice from the dense debris on the far side of the rubble-filled recess.

"Yeah, what do you think you are doing on our turf, pug dog?" uttered another threatening voice, this one coming from behind him.

PD Hood slowly raised his head and squared his square body, trying to act brave even while expecting to get whipped, whupped and worked over at any moment by whoever—or whatever—was with him here by the garbage pit. But while he was prepared for a fearsome sight, he was not expecting to be both frightened and moved by what he saw.

Closing in on little PD Hood from all around the dump were dozens of—*no,* he thought, *at least three hundred!*—skinny, sickly-looking dogs. Most were quite thin, some looked to have mange, some limped as if in pain, and others appeared just unwell in a way PD Hood could not quite define. And while some were posturing and acting tough, most, he thought, looked as scared as he felt.

In the hopes that maybe, just maybe, this wasn't about to be his final moment on Earth, PD Hood stiffened his spine and plucked deep for some pluckiness and said:

"Um, hi. I'm PD Hood. I'm from down the way in Dogville Digs."

The other dogs looked at one another—*incredulously?* thought PD Hood—and back at what they likely saw as an intruder.

PD Hood continued: "I came all the way here to see whether you dogs were real."

The thirty or so closest-in dogs looked like they didn't know whether to laugh or lunge. "What do you mean, real?" snapped a multi-hued mixed breed. "Obviously we are real, Mr. PD Hood the Nosy Pug."

"Yeah, Mr. Nosy Face, what do you want with us anyway?" demanded a dirt-covered Dalmatian. "We don't need any clean, fed, happily domesticated dogs encroaching on our territory! You probably just judge us and look down on us anyway!"

Before long, dozens of other strays had crowded in on PD Hood, joining in on the taunting and querying.

"Yeah, Mr. Perfect Pug! We do just fine here! We find our way! Don't you go putting us in your judgmental box, deciding we are no good!"

"Right! Just because you live in a fancy-pants house and get fancy-pants food doesn't make you better than us!"

"Exactly! We might not have toys, but we have each other! We find things to play with! Um, in the garbage, but still."

"Yes, and . . ." a mangy mastiff started, but then he stopped as he noticed PD Hood's hanging head. "Hey, hang on, you guys. I think he's crying."

The jeers and angry comments railing against little PD Hood suddenly ceased as the big dog leaned in toward the now shaking, weeping pug.

"Hey buddy, it's okay," the mastiff said. "Don't cry. We just are sorta territorial and suspicious of visitors."

"So tell us, what you are doing here?" the shabby mastiff continued. "No one ever visits us. Well, other than incoming new strays. None of the well-fed, well-kept town dogs do, that's for sure. And you're a town dog."

PD Hood, realizing he was not about to be the first fresh meat dinner these animals had enjoyed in some time, calmed down enough to speak.

"Okay . . ." he began. "As I mentioned, I'm PD Hood. I came because our chief elder Friar Foxhound and the other older dogs in our pack tell us stories—what we younger dogs have always assumed were mere tales—about alleged stray dogs at the landfill, dogs that don't have homes or regular meals or playthings.

"My buddy Little John Jämthund and I were talking about it just yesterday. We decided it had to be a myth, just some fabley folklore or something. But then I wondered why our elders would make something like that up, so . . . so here I am. I just had to see for myself whether uncared-for dogs really exist."

The filthy, foul-smelling dogs stared at the newcomer. A barrel-chested bulldog stepped forward. "Well, now you know. Now you can get out of here and go back to your warm house and your fancy food and toys. We don't need any townies coming around to remind us of what we will never have.

"Now go home!" growled the bulldog threateningly.

Not wanting to suffer harm, PD Hood turned to leave. But then a thought occurred to him: *Maybe I can help these poor dogs . . . Maybe I can make their lives better . . . I have a plan!*

"Hey, I have an idea," he quietly offered as the skeptical strays stared. "Maybe I can help you."

An angry-looking Airedale spoke up. "What do you mean, 'help' us? No town dogs have ever cared to help us!"

"Give me a chance. I'll be back," replied the suddenly excited PD Hood. As he raced off, the hundreds of stray dogs sat with their maws agape, wondering what on Earth the little pug meant.

That afternoon, PD Hood rushed over to Little John Jämthund's yard. He told his amazed amigo all about his trip to the landfill and the hundreds of stray dogs that resided there.

"It was so sad, Little John. So many were mangy, and others were lame, and most were so underweight. No one cares for them. No one loves them. No one brings them food."

And then PD Hood grinned the biggest snaggletooth grin and added:

"But we can change that! Little John, round up eight of the Merry Mutts and meet me at the dog park tomorrow at noon! We are going to help those dogs!!"

And off PD Hood went, racing home to plan out his "Save the Strays" strategy.

Meanwhile, down at Dogville City Hall, evil Sheriff Ralph the Dog was plotting a plan of his own. That morning, his loyal lieutenant Guy Greyhound reported espying PD Hood entering Dogville Dump while the greyhound was digging in the waste bins for trinkets to bring back to his boss.

"Your nemesis was nosing about!" Guy Greyhound had announced anxiously. "He now knows about the strays, those mutts you banished to the landfill when they no longer could pay their toy taxes and dog food duties!

"What if he reports you to Hound Palace?" the thin dog had thundered as he twisted and twirled in the sheriff's inner sanctum. "Prince Peter the Pomeranian will learn of all the toys and food you stole! You'll be sacked!! I'll be sacked!!"

"Not to worry, Guy," Sheriff Ralph the Dog had responded confidently. "Trust me, Prince Peter will learn no such thing. Our jobs—and all our copped kibble, poached playthings and other nicked numnums—aren't going anywhere."

The next morning, the unjust justice was grinning from flappy ear to flappy ear. He had just put the final flourishes on two new laws: one declaring that PD Hood would see an immediate doubling of his already tripled taxation for "Dogville Dump trespassing" and a second law decreeing the same fate for any Dogville Digs resident caught entering the landfill in the future.

As he pressed his paw on an ink pad and then stamped the parchment of a proclamation, wicked Sheriff Ralph the Dog pushed aside any worries Guy Greyhound had planted in him the day prior and imagined his growing stores of food and toys—true dog wealth by any measure.

If PD Hood doesn't want himself and his maddening Merry Mutts to end up residing in that dump, he will keep his maw muffled about the strays and mind his own business! thought Sheriff Ralph the Dog. *And certainly no other dog is going to risk a rise in taxes just to enter a dump.*

His sinister sneer widened. *My job is as secure as the new lock I will put on the dump gate once I tax that annoying PD Hood right out of Dogville Digs and into a life at the landfill,* he mused.

That same day, PD Hood arrived at Dogville Dog Park to find a nonet of eager-looking Merry Mutts waiting for him. Little John Jämthund had filled them in on PD Hood's travels and about the reality of the stray dogs and about PD having an idea for how to help them.

"Thanks for coming," PD Hood began. "If you saw what I saw yesterday, you'd understand the urgency of what we are about to do. Those dogs need our help.

"Here's my plan. It occurred to me that while we dogs of Dogville Digs have *some* food we could share, the dogs at Dogville Estates have so much more! They have endless food, extra treats, and more toys than they can keep track of! They certainly won't notice if a bit here and there goes missing, right? So my idea is we, um, borrow kibble, cookies and toys from the rich dogs and redistribute them to the poor dogs at the dump who have nothing!"

"Genius!" blurted Bernard Beagle.

"Masterful!" chimed in Charlie Chihuahua.

"Love it!" added Alfie Afghan Hound.

That night, PD Hood and his Merry Mutts stealthily entered Dogville Estates. They hopped fences and waited by the backdoors with large sacks as Charlie Chihuahua quietly slipped in through the flap of each doggie door and then undid the front door locks and bolts. One house after another, PD Hood and his friends took kibble, goodies, toys and even blankets from the rich dogs' homes.

"Do you think they'll notice?" a nervous Nellie Newfoundland asked PD Hood. "I mean, we must have fifty pounds of kibble here, and dozens of blankets, and, gosh, hundreds of toys and cookies and other goodies. What if we get caught? We're taking a big risk."

PD Hood looked incredulous. "Risk? It's the poor starving dogs who are at risk—at risk of getting sick, or worse! We have to help them! These Dogville Estates hounds' hoards are huge! They'll never notice!"

The other dogs wagged their tails in agreement. Even nervous Nellie Newfoundland overcame her worry and tail-wagged away.

As the night went on, PD Hood and his pals sorted the goods—kibble, treats, toys and blankets—and grouped them in multiple bags. Each dog shouldered as many bags as it could carry—from one bag on little Charlie Chihuahua's wee body all the way to eight bags on the back of Graham Great Dane. Their loot loaded, off the Merry Mutts headed to the landfill.

Meanwhile, the strays had tried to forget about PD Hood and his promise to help, so accustomed were they to disappointment. After all, life for them had been nothing but struggle and want ever since that corrupt cur Sheriff Ralph the Dog had forced them to give up their homes and live in the landfill because they were unable to keep up with annual increases in toy and treat taxes.

So each and every one of the landfill dogs was completely shocked when, at the stroke of midnight, in marched ten town dogs laden with what looked like dozens and dozens of overfilled bags.

"I'm back!" PD Hood exclaimed, expressing the obvious. "These are my friends; they helped me get you some stuff I think you'll like!"

The strays slowly, warily, cautiously gathered around the sack-laden visitors. PD Hood and his comrades quickly shed their loads, all looking excitedly at the equally eager denizens of the dump.

And then in unison, the PD gang opened the sacks, exposing the loot, and shouted, "*Tada!*"

The strays stood stock still, unable to believe their eyes. Never had they seen such largesse—a largesse of love—as this. Inside the wide-open bags were gobs of dry dog food, hundreds of cookies, scores of fun-looking toys, and piles of warm blankets. The homeless dogs could not stop staring. Not one of them moved.

Finally a Siberian husky—who was anything but husky thanks to a lifetime of insufficient meals—snapped out of his trance and looked at PD and his team.

"I'm Simon the Siberian Husky," he quietly said in a choked-up voice. "I'm not sure what to say, PD Hood. Why did you do this? Where is it all from? Why did you help us? No one helps us. We only get punished and abandoned."

PD's snaggletooth poked through his gigantic grin. "Well, it's simple math, Simon. You needed food and toys, and we got you food and toys."

"But from whom? From where?" the husky asked, his expression a warring combination of hope that the goodies were genuine and doubt that they truly were for him and his impoverished friends.

"Oh, don't you fret about that," PD Hood said with a wink. "Just enjoy our gifts to you! And . . . eat up! There's more where this came from!"

And with that, PD Hood and his band of well-meaning plunderers took off toward home.

The next day, after spending the morning fine-tuning his "Save the Strays" campaign, PD Hood again called a meeting of his Merry Mutts crew.

"Here's the deal, you guys," he said. "We did a great thing! The poor stray dogs finally have real food and toys and blankets. But there are so many of them, the food we dropped off yesterday won't last long. And the Dogville Estates dogs didn't even notice that anything was missing. So: Let's go again! Tonight after dark! Who's in?"

But even before any member of the Merry Mutts responded, PD Hood sensed something had changed. There was a definite shift—a downward dip—in their excitement level. PD Hood's googly eyes traveled from one end of the group of downward-gazing dogs to the other, trying to ascertain what had them so discouraged.

Keeping their heads bowed low, not meeting their leader's gaze, the Merry Mutts all slowly, hesitantly raised a forepaw—all but little Charlie Chihuahua. Instead of raising a paw, the tiny dog did a tiny gulp and raised his head.

"Oh, PD Hood," he said sorrowfully, "we do want to help the strays. We truly do." Charlie Chihuahua looked at the other dogs, all of whom lifted their heads and nodded in agreement. Then he took a big breath and went on. "But while you were locked away planning out today's pillaging program, Sheriff Ralph the Dog's henchman Guy Greyhound was racing about Dogville Digs! He was posting a new proclamation from the sheriff, and . . ."

Little John Jämthund stepped forward and took over the relaying of the bad news.

"It's really terrible," PD Hood's sidekick said, staring into the widening googly eyes of their friend and leader. "It's an official proclamation, stamped by the sheriff. It says that as punishment for your having entered Dogville Dump, your taxes are being doubled. And that's not all! It says any other Dogville Digs dog caught at the dump will suffer the same fate!"

Charlie Chihuahua again spoke up. "So we were talking about it when you came in, and . . . PD Hood? Are you sure we are doing the right thing?"

The Merry Mutts looked at one another, the dilemma clearly weighing heavily on their minds.

Alfie Afghan stepped forward. "Look, Little John; look, Charlie. Those strays have no one else to help them. Without us, they will have to keep scavenging forever. PD's plan is saving them from a continued life of barely surviving. And those rich dogs in Dogville Estates sure won't notice a few toys and some food going missing.

"So are you guys in or not?"

Charlie Chihuahua looked around at the encouraging faces of his pals, all of whom were nodding their furry heads at him with their paws in the air, expressing approval.

"Oh, okay," Charlie Chihuahua said, looking more sure of things. "I'm in! Let's save dogs!"

PD Hood clearly was moved; pretending to cough, he averted his large pug head and quickly wiped a tear with his forepaw. Turning back, he saw that Charlie Chihuahua and the rest of the Merry Mutts were looking decidedly merrier by the moment, excited once again because the "Save the Strays" plan was back on track with unanimous support.

"Are you all certain you want to do this?" PD Hood asked them. "I am already an outlaw in the eyes of Sheriff Ralph the Dog. My taxes likely will always go up, up, up until one day I will be unable to pay my annual levy, and I'll find myself banished to the junkyard, a neighbor of our new friends. But the rest of you need to think about what you're saying. If you get caught, you too will face the sheriff's taxation wrath."

All as one, the Merry Mutts rolled their eyes. "Are those button ears hard of hearing?" Christopher Cockapoo said laughingly. "We said we're in!"

Each night for the next week, PD Hood and his band of bandits burgled the pantries and toy baskets of the homes in Dogville Estates and carried the plunder to the landfill, where the grateful strays were finally getting full bellies and enjoying playtime with plush playthings—some of them for the first time in their lives.

PD Hood and his Merry Mutts were careful to take just enough that the well-to-do dogs would not notice the reduction in their food and toys. PD Hood, having seen the regular deliveries of countless bags and boxes from PetSmart and Petco over the years, reasoned that the kibble, treats, balls and blankets they, er, relocated would quickly be replenished.

They'll never know, PD assured himself. *It's fine. It's a good thing we are doing. A good thing!*

A month passed. And what a difference a mere month made. The dogs of the dump for the first time looked almost as healthy as the dogs of the village. They never could have imagined laughing like they were now; they played like they'd only ever played in their dreams. With the help of his band of brothers, PD Hood was changing lives. And the strays were sure to let him know every time he came—now three times a week due to there being enough extra food at this point to store it in a big bin PD had 'found' in a Dogville Estates backyard.

"There were two bins in that yard, you guys," he had told a worried-looking Little John Jämthund and Perry the Poodle. "Who needs *two* bins?"

Over the next many weeks, the "redistribution" continued. And, sure enough, they did end up "borrowing" that second bin; there were too many toys and blankets at that point to let them just pile up in the elements.

"No one wants wet toys and blankets, Little John!" PD Hood justified to his second-in-command, who wagged his long, slightly curled Jämthund tail.

"You got that right, pal," his friend replied. "And, wow, some of the toys still had tags! And two of the blankets were that rare vicuña wool I've seen on the Home Shopping Network."

"Well, remember, these dogs need love, and we are, um, letting the Dogville Estates dogs, um, offer love," PD Hood said. Then he added with a wink, "I know they'd be happy to help!"

PD Hood's "Save the Strays" plan entered its third month. All was going so well! The "visits" to the upscale homes were so surreptitiously executed, and the number of toys, bags of food, and other items taken so perfectly planned, that the absence of the items went unnoticed.

"Save the Strays" truly is working, PD Hood thought with pride as he, Little John Jämthund and Dennis Doberman headed one late night to a particularly huge mansion they'd yet to explore. *We are doing so much good, giving so much help to the poor, neglected dogs. Good! Good! Good!*

In fact, PD Hood and his Merry Mutts were so confident that their acts of charity were right and noble that—as they were about to slip the doggie door of yet another manse—it never occurred to them that something so "right" could one day go wrong.

Until it did.

PD Hood's round head squeezed through the flap in the door, and then he froze—half his body in, half out.

"Oooof!!" exclaimed Dennis Doberman as his snout butted into PD's backside.

"Yowch!!" yipped Little John Jämthund as he, in turn, smacked his face into the dobie's rump.

The only one *not* making a sound was PD Hood—because, directly in front of him, blocking him from coming into the grand home, was a borzoi who apparently was answering a nocturnal weewee urge.

"Hey! You! What do you think you're doing trying to get into my house?" the surprised and now territorial borzoi demanded. "And why do you have a big bag?"

Gobsmacked, and with his googly eyes so wide he feared they'd pop out of their sockets, PD Hood quickly if awkwardly reversed course, pushing his no-longer-bag-holding upper body and large head back outside, ramming his bum into a confused Dennis Doberman—who dominoed his own rump into poor, confused Little John Jämthund as he went.

Sensing that now was not the time to ask questions, the alarmed duo abandoned their sacks and raced away from the manor, PD close at their heels. The bandit buddies bolted down the lush lawn and thought they'd made a successful getaway when *smack!*—they bashed one after another into a veritable wall of Dogville Estates dogs. The line of fierce-faced hounds stared them down, silently daring them to attempt to pass.

"Yeah! Good job, guys!" called a voice from behind them. They turned to see the borzoi from the manor. "Yeah, that's right," he sneered at PD and his pals. "I whistled to them so they'd block your escape! I saw a bunch of mystery middle-income town dogs sniffing around our neighborhood a few nights ago and wondered what was going on!

"Now, you have about five seconds to tell us what the likes of you are doing in Dogville Estates! Start talking, pug dog, or my next dog whistle will be to the office of Sheriff Ralph the Dog!"

By now, Charlie Chihuahua, Bernard Beagle, Alfie Afghan Hound and the rest of the PD Hood pack had come to the scene, having wondered what was keeping their friends so long. PD Hood's gang rotated their heads from their leader to the Dogville Estates–guarding canines, waiting to hear his explanation.

Fearing the jig was up but hopeful these Dogville Estates dogs might understand the rationale for this redistribution operation, this "Save the Strays" plan, PD Hood decided the truth was the best way to go.

"Well, see," PD Hood began as dozens of dog eyes stared, "turns out what we—and probably you, too—thought were just old dogs' tales about stray dogs living in Dogville Dump weren't just made-up stories, courtesy of Friar Foxhound and the rest of the elders."

"What?!" blared the borzoi. "That's silly! Of course it's a myth! There can't be homeless dogs with no food or love! Even middle-class Dogville dogs have a place to call home.

And food to eat. And at least a toy or two. Stop trying to fool us! Tell us why you're *really* here!"

"Well, that's just it!" PD Hood said. "That *is* why we are here. Sadly, Friar Foxhound was telling the truth; the strays are very real . . ."

PD Hood proceeded to tell the Dogville Estates dogs all about the past three months, from his curiosity-fueled foray to the landfill to see for himself the existence of the hungry homeless mutts to his launching of the "Save the Strays" campaign to the . . .

"Wait! What?" yelled an enraged Pekingese from the far end of the dog wall. "You stole our stuff?! You took kibble? And our cookies? And our blankets? Thieves! You all are thieves!!

"Tell me right now why we shouldn't drag you by your tails straight to Sheriff Ralph the Dog and tell him you stole our stuff! He'll tax you clear into tomorrow! Clear into a life in the landfill! You'll be in bad trouble! You'll—"

"Wait, hang on, Peter," the borzoi said to the Pekingese. Turning to PD Hood, he said: "Let me get this straight. You discovered the strays, saw that they needed food and toys and other help, and then, to help them, you figured you were justified in taking from the rich to give to the poor? That we 'hoity-toity' wealthy dogs could afford to give some of our food and toys away to destitute dogs?"

PD Hood looked sheepishly at the borzoi and then from one end of the dog wall—which had grown by dozens more Dogville Estates canines and now extended down the block—to the other.

"Er, sorta," PD Hood replied, staring at his forepaws to avoid what he was certain was disapproval at best, attack stance at worst. "See . . . you are rich dogs. All we did was, um, redistribute a little of your overage to the poor dogs, the dogs with nothing. Surely you don't want dogs having nothing . . . ?"

PD Hood and his pals feared the worst as the rich dogs formed a circle and appeared to be having a conference. They whispered amongst themselves for several minutes, glancing over at the PD Hood posse every now and then. Finally, the circle broke apart and the wealthy dogs again approached the pug and his friends.

"Bobby," a Scottish terrier said, addressing the borzoi, "none of us can bear to imagine dogs without any food or toys. And I for one have a never-ending supply of kibble, cookies and other treats. I have more toys than I could ever play with. I must have a dozen blankets that—in my heated home—I don't really even need.

"I'm happy to share . . . although, okay, I wish I'd had a vote on this 'Save the Strays' redistribution plan. But I'm not mad; I *like* that I've helped starving dogs." He stared at PD Hood. "Even if I didn't know I was doing it."

Suddenly, breaking the tension, one of the Dogville Estates dogs started laughing, and then another. Then a third started guffawing so hard he was clutching his belly. Soon the whole group of affluent dogs had joined in the chuckling and chortling.

The laughter finally died down as one teacup poodle dog raised her dainty, well-heeled heel and addressed the bandits' ringleader.

"PD Hood, I'm Penelope Teacup Poodle," said the very smiley white-furred dog. "My pal Brenda Border Collie and I just the other day were actually complaining—*complaining*, if you can believe it!—that our toy baskets were too full and it was hard to find our favorites. And we were both grousing because we had accidentally bought generic brand packages of cookies!"

"Exactly," Brenda Border Collie chimed in. "I mean, there we were griping and grumbling about having too much, when meanwhile there are hundreds of dogs with absolutely nothing.

"We all want to help. We all have enough to share. But, PD Hood . . ." And here the border collie looked at Bobby Borzoi to let him finish expressing what the Dogville Estates canines had collectively concluded.

The now grinning borzoi stepped forward. "Yeah, next time," he said, addressing PD Hood and his friends, "just ask. We wouldn't mind. We *are* kinda spoiled. We are happy to share our loot."

That night, PD Hood, his crew and all his new Dogville Estates buddies entered the Dogville Dump. Upon seeing the hundreds of dogs—better fed than three months ago, but still thin and mangy—the wealthy dogs were moved to tears.

And from that day forward, the Dogville Estates dogs happily helped PD Hood feed the dogs—dogs who soon were no longer homeless, thanks to the Dogville Doghousing Project, funded by Dogville Estates.

And despite Sheriff Ralph the Dog finally catching on to the goings-on at the landfill, his greedy paws were tied. He faced a daunting dilemma: Arrest PD Hood and risk the pug's exposing his vault of plundered playthings and ill-gotten grub while also risking the wrath of the Estate dogs that funded his bi-annual campaigns? Or let the strays be cared for, reduce PD Hood's tax rate, stop overtaxing the poor and middle-class canines, and at least stay in office?

It was a no-brainer. *Fine,* the sinister sheriff sniffed sneeringly. *PD Hood won't see the punishment I'd gladly mete out, but at least I'll remain in charge of the Homeland of Hound and rule Dogville and the other domains.*

But, sadly for Sheriff Ralph the Dog, there was about to be a new sheriff in town—er, in the Homeland of Hound.

Unbeknownst to the greedy lawman, his underling Guy Greyhound—who resided in Dogville Estates and was the beau of Brenda Border Collie—had had a change of heart. The sheriff's lieutenant had also assumed the role of Bobby Borzoi's helper, overseeing the food, toy and blanket donations. And just recently, a certain Merry Mutt had "suggested" the greyhound would make a fine sheriff come the next election cycle. Charlie Chihuahua was named campaign manager, and the Merry Mutts and their Dogville Estates buddies began writing up Guy Greyhound's election promises, the first of which, of course, was greatly lowered taxes for the poor and middle classes.

Meanwhile, PD Hood's "Save the Strays" plan continued to be an overwhelming success. Even if PD had needed a lesson in proper and improper "redistribution."

(PD note: This PD Fairy Tail is based on the legend of Robin Hood and His Merry Men. The moral of the story is that we should help those in need, stand up for what is right, and fight injustice. Well, yeah, but also, Mommy needs to budget—and maybe get second and third jobs—to be able to buy kibble and toys and treats and other stuff for stray dogs. And also take the strays to the vet. And also let them live in our house.)

EPILOGUE

Prince PD and the beautiful Fawn Girl Pug are dancing the night away when suddenly the clock strikes midnight. The fair maiden pug widens her gorgeous googly eyes and races away, but not before a glass slipper slips off her dainty hind paw . . .

"I will find her! I will marry her!" Prince PD promises himself as he picks up the dainty glass shoe and sets off to find the paw on which it fits, visions of his happy life with Fawn Girl Pug, of their palatial doghouse, of their ten puppies filling his mind with joy. All his dreams are about to come true, and . . .

"PD? PD, wake up honey." Mommy's face is inches from mine as she gently rubs my belly, rousing me from my snooze. "Silly boy, I think you might have dozed off right at the part where the prince was about to marry Cinderella. But I can back up a bit and catch you up, okay?"

Catch me up? Catch me up? I am the one who should catch you up, Mommy! Catch you and the Cinderella author up on how to properly write this tale, I think as I try and hold onto the remnants of the delightful dream I was pulled away from. My sweet sojourn to Love La-la Land, where I finally was about to live in wedded bliss forever and ever and ever with my secret fawn girl pug crush. So happy, so in love . . .

Alas, I'm back in Realville: glass-slipper-less, fawn-girl-pug-less, blissful-future-less, and still dealing with that mutt Ralph trying to move in on my maiden. Okay, the maiden who I still haven't pugged up and manned up and met yet. And having to be treated for "anxiety" I don't have!

As Mommy thumbs back a few pages to repeat what I missed while napping, I jump down from the ottoman and pad over to my empty food bowl. I peer in, hopeful that somehow I miraculously left a kibble or two in there from dinner. Apparently my romantic dream has caused me to work up a bit of an appetite.

Of course, I *am* a pug. *Everything* works up my appetite. Sadly, said pug appetite generally does not result in leftovers after meals to find later; regrettably, my bowl per usual is licked clean.

"Oh, I see," Mommy says, smiling as she rises, then walks to the drawer where she keeps some PD goodies and bully sticks and slides it open. "Does the prince of *this* castle want a treat?"

She digs through a little bowl and pulls out a frosted Milk Bone, then does her silly raised hand thingy to get me to "sit."

I perform my trained monkey trick and park my fur-covered caboose on the hardwood floor and give a big snagglegrin, hoping my indescribable cuteness will lead to a second snack. Alas, it's one and done; Mommy tosses me the goodie and then slides the treat treasure trove shut and resettles on the cuddle chair, patting the seat next to her.

"C'mere, Prince PD," she says, waggling the storybook. "Let's finish the tale and find out what happens to Cinderella! I'm so excited, aren't you?"

Oh, very well, Mommy, I think as I leap onto her lap. *Let's finish this runner-up to my correct version of this tale and put me to bed, where I can continue refashioning fables.*

I'll pretend I love this book and this fairy tale time in general. I'll act all calm, and I won't chew things that aren't my bully sticks or toys, and I won't potty inside or do anything else to make Mommy and the vet thinking I need a dog shrink.

Because I don't. And it's my ability to rewrite a fairy tale, my talent for making a fable more fabulous, that has shown me how to overcome what Mommy perceives as anxiousness.

Starting tomorrow, starting with our first walkie of the new day, no more just marking bushes while Ralph makes time with my girl! No! In my new, better-written, better-done version of *me,* of the life of PD the Pug, I will be *brave!* I will *meet her!* I will have her as *my own!*

And then, someday soon . . . Prince PD and his real-life Cinderella, a.k.a. my—no longer secret!—fawn girl pug crush and I will wave goodbye to that junkyard rubbish Ralph as we set off in our carriage for a palace fit for a pug. Or, okay, Mommy's house. But still, me and my princess, living a fairy tale come true. Written and achieved by Bard and Prince PD the Pug.

(PD note: Um, maybe a session or two with that dog shrink for how to approach her. . . .)

GET IN TOUCH WITH PD!

You can write to him at

PD the Pug Productions
2200 Wilson Boulevard
Suite 102-265
Arlington, VA 22201

Or give him a shout at

pdthepug@gmail.com

ABOUT THE AUTHOR

Not since the Bard himself dipped his feathered quill in his inkwell has a writer so wowed the literary world.

In 2021, the release of PD the Pug's first masterpiece, *Get Me Out of Here! Reflections of PD the Put-Upon Pug*, introduced the wordsmith wunderhund who has gone on to become the planet's most prodigious pug.

It has been one crowd-pleaser after another with the publication of *No, YOU Sit! PD the Pug's Manual for How to Train Your Human, Working Like a . . . Dog! PD the Pug in Corporate America*, and *A Star Is Born! PD the Pug on the Silver Screen*. And as PD's latest work of genius rolls off the printing presses, book reviewers already are using superlatives generally reserved for only the luminaries of literature.

While being a five-time dog author is amazing, astonishing and astounding, PD's impressive resume goes far beyond his mastery of the written word.

He has been inducted into the Flying Furbaby Federation for most times landing on his head while chasing squirrels up trees; he has earned a gold medal in the Dog Olympics' "Longest Zoomies" category; he remains uncontested as the

Digging-Almost-To-China competition champion; he is the nation's top tail chaser, winning the esteemed Dizzy Dog trophy for spinning seventeen times in one twirl; and he thrice achieved the upper limit of the decibel scale while whining for an extra cookie from Mommy.

A descendant of a breed that once was treasured by, and a companion to, Chinese royalty, PD has enjoyed a not-quite-royal yet very spoiled life in the suburbs of Washington, DC with his doting and beloved Mommy since she adopted him six years ago from Howling Hill Kennels.

To let PD know your thoughts on how he has changed the literary landscape, email him at pdthepug@gmail.com. You can also follow him on Instagram and Facebook at @pdthepug and visit PD online at PDThePugProductions.com.

Furry Fairy Tails is PD's fifth book.

ABOUT MOMMY

Mommy Marilee Joyce is honored to have her own room in PD the Pug's Arlington, Virginia home. Mommy's privileges include feeding, walking, and bathing him; getting the goopies out of his googly eyes; cleaning up his whoopsies; Q-tipping his ears and nose fold; and explaining that it is merely his reflection he is barking at in the sliding glass door and not a threat to the household, his toys, or his treats.

When not caring for or playing with PD, Mommy is running Joyce Communications and PD the Pug Productions. Mommy has served as an anchor and reporter for several television affiliates. In Washington, she has produced and hosted several television programs from Capitol Hill, and her company currently offers full video and audio production services.

Mommy is grateful with each new sunrise that she has been blessed with PD. And she is amazed and astounded that her shenanigans-seeking, antics-attracting, tomfoolery-trolling little pug is so bright and brainy. In fact, as this book went to press, Mommy espied her little PD already working on his sixth book. . . .

OTHER WORKS BY PD THE PUG

Get Me Out Of Here! Reflections of PD the Put-Upon Pug

*No, YOU Sit! PD the Pug's Manual
for How to Train Your Human*

Working Like A . . . Dog! PD the Pug in Corporate America

A Star Is Born! PD the Pug on the Silver Screen

www.ingramcontent.com/pod-product-compliance
Lightning Source LLC
Chambersburg PA
CBHW071748120626
46550CB00002B/705